"The Christian Church is full of u
the Bible assures us, will be a d
those unsung heroes are reveale
kingdom. The name Leslie Land is possibly a name you have never
heard. Until Ian Shaw wrote an article on Pastor Land's life in a
recent Banner of Truth Magazine, I had never heard his name.
And yet, Land exercised a fruitful and richly blessed ministry, was
a much prized friend of Martyn Lloyd Jones, and held fast to the
gospel of grace at a time when liberalism and ecumenism were
infecting the life of the church in England. Ian Shaw's engaging
biography will hold your attention, remind you of the gospel
faithfulness that God honours, and impress on you the godly virtue of being an unsung hero. I am delighted to commend this brief
but richly instructive biography."

Ian Hamilton
President,
Westminster Presbyterian Theological Seminary

"This is my kind of biography. Rich, instructive, edifying—and of
a saint of God, who was tremendously used in his day, but who,
for various reasons, has been forgotten, even though he passed
from the scene of history only recently.

I first came across the name of Leslie Land through Ian Shaw's
fine study of his friendship with the Reformed colossus of the
twentieth century, D. Martyn Lloyd-Jones. Obviously long familiar with Dr. Lloyd-Jones, I was intrigued by an area of the Doctor's
life I knew nothing about and also because of the topic of friendship. That study has now blossomed into this really tremendous
biography, which I heartily commend to all who love the encouragement that can be derived especially from Christian biography."

Michael A.G. Haykin
Chair & Professor of Church History,
The Southern Baptist Theological Seminary

"Ian Shaw has lovingly recovered the memory of a life that was in
danger of being forgotten: that of the mid-20th century minister
W. Leslie Land. Dr. Shaw has woven together from scattered historical sources a record of Land's life and, in particular, his

ministry at Melbourne Hall in Leicester. The notes of Land's sermons in the second half of the book provide a stimulating insight into the biblical, doctrinal and experiential content of his preaching. The result is an account of this man of God which is both instructive in the context of church life in Britain in the middle years of the last century and an inspiring example to ministers, preachers and Christians today."

Robert Strivens
Pastor, Bradford on Avon Baptist Church

"Leslie Land is one of those gems in church history that are easy to ignore, especially because, as a self-effacing pastor, he was quick to draw the attention away from himself and onto Christ. Yet, in a society (and often a church) that gravitates towards celebrities, Land is someone we need to know in order to balance our lives and expectations. I am grateful to Ian Shaw for bringing Land's life to light. In this well-written and carefully-researched book, readers will discover a man who quietly influenced his generation—including his good friend Martyn Lloyd-Jones—in profound, lasting, and often unexpected ways."

Simonetta Carr
Author of the series
Christian Biographies for Young Readers

"I thoroughly enjoyed Ian Shaw's warm and engaging biography of Leslie Land, and applaud his decision to bring Land's life out of the shadows to share with the wider evangelical community. I was naturally particularly touched by Shaw's chapter on Land's friendship with my grandfather, Martyn Lloyd-Jones, for whom Christian friendships were a bedrock of support during his time in the ministry. I do hope that everyone who has an interest in the lives of Godly men in the last century will avail themselves of the opportunity to get to know Leslie Land better in Ian's masterful biography."

Jonathan F. Catherwood
Former President,
the MLJ Trust

IAN SHAW

LESLIE LAND
His Life and Ministry

press

Leslie Land: His Life and Ministry

Joshua Press (an imprint of H&E Publishing), West Lorne, Ontario
www.joshuapress.com

Cover and layout design by Chance Faulkner
Front cover image: "New Walk in 1951." Used by kind permission of "Story of Leicester" https://storyofleicester.info

Paperback ISBN: 978-1-77484-114-3
eBook ISBN: 978-1-77484-115-0

Contents

LIFE

Chapter 1
Encountering Leslie Land

The English Midlands—the very name suggests something rather unexceptional and ordinary. Bordering one another you can find Northamptonshire and Leicestershire, the kind of counties that most people who have spent their lives in Britain, if asked to locate them, would stab the map somewhere in the centre and hope for the best. Yet within these boundaries eighteenth and nineteenth century Christians could find John Newton, slave ship captain, letter and hymn-writer and latterly supporter of William Wilberforce in his work against the slave trade. Also, Andrew Fuller, who spent much of his life in the Northamptonshire town of Kettering, and William Carey, born in Northamptonshire and living in Leicester before leaving for the mission field in India. Two other Northampton Johns—Sutcliff and Ryland—made Carey's sustained ministry possible.[1]

Stepping forward to the twentieth century we encounter W. Leslie Land, a man whose life and ministry mirrored this earlier concern for faithful preaching, pastoral care, and the mission field. In the years immediately following the Second World War he brought to the city of Leicester a ministry that exemplified the revival of reformed Evangelicalism that took

---

[1] Michael Haykin, *One Heart and One Soul: John Sutcliff of Olney, his Friends and Times* (Darlington: Evangelical Press, 1994) gives a valuable background. John R. Todd, *By the Foolishness of Preaching* (Barton in the Beans Baptist Church, 1983), is a now hard to find brief account of Leicestershire and the 18th century Evangelical Revival. On John Newton, in addition to various readily obtainable biographies, the John Newton Project, led by Marylynn Rose, is an invaluable resource (www.johnnewton.org).

place initially in England, Scotland, Wales, and North America.

Early in the 1950s a middle-aged man sat for the first time in Melbourne Hall, a church in the city of Leicester almost at the centre of England, gripped by preaching and teaching that were a revelation to him. Isaac Mountenay decided that such a ministry demanded a record. He could be seen carrying what seventy years ago was euphemistically called a "portable" tape recorder, to begin one of the earliest Christian audio recording projects. The church soon opened a recording studio that for its time was state of the art, with the result that today recordings still exist of Sunday and weeknight messages delivered by W. Leslie Land.

Leaving his position as head of Seaford College, a private school in Sussex,[2] Leslie Land had moved, *via* a short ministry on the south coast of England, to Melbourne Hall in Leicester in 1947. There he commenced a fourteen-year ministry that was to prove more far reaching than any period in that church since F.B. Meyer became its first minister late in the nineteenth century.

The events and people we know about and remember from our national histories say much about how we see ourselves today—or wish to be seen. Christians are not immune from this, and much good writing has endeavoured to provide a corrective to our forgetfulness.[3] However, Leslie Land (1903–1986)

---

[2] Founded in 1884, Leslie Land was the fifth Headteacher of Seaford College, from 1935-1944, having been appointed to the post in his early thirties. In 1940, early in the Second World War, the school was requisitioned by government order and evacuated to Worthing, at a time when threat of German invasion was very real. Famous former pupils who would have known Leslie Land included Hugh Bentall, a pioneer of open-heart surgery, and Louis Blom-Cooper, a famous lawyer.

[3] For example, Michael Haykin has sought to restore to the light of day the lives and work of the evangelical Calvinists within the British Baptist community in the period bridging the eighteenth and nineteenth centuries.

apparently had few family members who knew his life, and no biographer. Despite being encouraged to do so, he wrote nothing for publication, and left only faint traces on the spiritual landscape. After leaving Melbourne Hall in his late fifties he quickly disappeared from view, before dying following a long illness in the mid-1980s.

Tracing his life is like a jigsaw puzzle with many missing pieces. "William Leslie Land, born 20 January 1903 at Wirksworth; son of Samuel Land, retired Draper and Outfitter. Educated at the Grammar School, Wirksworth. Admitted 1 March 1921." So reads the Christ's College, Cambridge, Admissions Book. Wirksworth was a Derbyshire town that had not too long before been the second town in the county, with its wealth founded on the lead mining industry. It had fallen on lean times by the end of the nineteenth century. Land's father came from a line of lead miners but had established what seems to have been a successful business. At the time of the 1911 Census there were two servants living in their house along with Leslie's older brother Eric, later to be minister at Worthing, and a boarding relative who was head teacher of the Coalville Elementary School. Leslie's mother, Minnie, was a schoolteacher. His parents were committed members of the local Baptist church and his father occasionally preached there.

The Old Grammar School, Wirksworth

Speaking in 1949 on "Why Isn't Everybody a Christian Believer?" he made a rare reference to becoming a Christian. Speaking of the church he attended he said,

> I could "hear and hear" gospel sermons, perhaps preached with the very heart-blood and passion of a consecrated preacher, but I could gaily persist in withholding my ... heart, the yielding of which would have involved a radical revolution in my pitiable self-centred existence.
>
> But the time came—I cannot tell you the day or the hour; I cannot relate a crisis or give an exciting testimony—the time came when Jesus "came alive" and real to me: I *heard* the gospel message, really *heard* it, listened in to it with my whole being, gave my God-roused imagination to it. I felt—I still do feel my heart beat a little

faster whenever I hear or preach the gospel of the re-deeming love of God in Jesus Christ. "All within me leaps to greet Thee" ... I looked and looked, and now I saw Calvary as the place where *my* sin and *my* self-centred life were crucified and put away for ever ... *I shall never forget the sight! I shall never forget the sight!* And I shall go on telling, in different ways and in different idioms, of this saving, this dynamic, explosive love of God in Jesus Christ, in the hope, no in the simple faith that every time I tell it—backed up by the prayers of a praying people—someone here, someone there, by the impact of God's Spirit, will be stirred out of their ease and complacency in sin...

What was it, you say, that held me back so long? Oh, it was self-centredness ... so entombed in my ego-centred outlook and sin; fooling about in the basement of life.[4]

Leslie matriculated to Cambridge University, on 22 October 1921, having been admitted to Christ's College. He studied Chemistry, Physics and Mathematics for the Natural Sciences Tripos. He graduated BA on 24 June 1924 and MA on 20 January 1928.[5] He taught science at Seaford for some years (in the words of a former colleague, "a very good science teacher according to his past pupils") before being appointed Headmaster of the College in 1935.

The school's ethos was strongly Christian. Joscelyn Johnson, once his young colleague, mentions that the Chapel Notes in the school magazine recorded the names of visiting preachers. The record of the July 10, 1943, Speech Day notes "Prizes

---

[4] Unless mentioned otherwise, this and subsequent quotations are from the substantial monthly magazine of Melbourne Hall. Mary Ward gave me copies of the magazine covering all but three of the fourteen years he was at Melbourne Hall.

[5] Information provided by University Archives, Cambridge University.

presented by Dr. Martyn Lloyd-Jones." This was not the first time. We know from the correspondence between him and Lloyd-Jones that he first spoke at the School in July 1939. Other visiting speakers included George Carey (later to be Archbishop of Canterbury), and well-known names of the time such as Rev. Basil Mowll, David Tryon, and Leslie's older brother, Eric Land, who was minister of Worthing Tabernacle, Ernest Kevan, then Principal of the London Bible College,[6] and numerous others whose appear here and there in the pages of this book. Joscelyn Johnson recalls:

> Mr Land was an excellent musician. He had found a Hammond (electrical) organ for the school in the 1930s ... He explained its properties to me and I accompanied him on it at the daily services, morning and evening.

He was man of remarkable gifts. A friend recalled "it was wonderful to hear him play; he could have been a classical pianist—he was very good." He continued: "I got him, I think it was Schubert's *Impromptu*. Certainly pretty difficult. I said, 'Do you know that Leslie?' He said, 'I cut my teeth on it!'" He was also an artist of no mean talent. The same friend remembers, "He came down to Torquay when we were there on one occasion ... My wife said I saw him on the seafront, and he was—he'd got his easel—he was drawing ... on the seafront at Torquay."

He was a man of remarkable natural ability in different fields. A member of the church later recalled Leslie Land singing a solo after preaching in the evening on one occasion "in

---

[6] For readers unfamiliar with Ernest Kevan, Paul Brown, *Ernest Kevan: Leader in Twentieth Century British Evangelicalism* (Edinburgh: Banner of Truth Trust, 2012), gives a useful overview.

his fine baritone voice." "Jesus and shall it ever be a mortal man ashamed of Thee" is one solo recalled by his church members. Paul Bassett, a later minister of Melbourne Hall, writes "I shall never forget his walking in from the garden in Worthing, sitting down in his open-necked shirt and grey flannels and nonchalantly playing Grieg's Piano Concerto." [7]

Land coped with the evacuation and resettlement of the school during the Second World War. This was a difficult period, with the school divided between three buildings, limited facilities, restrictions on movement, and fuel shortages—yet there was, as one former pupil recalled, "a great feeling of friendship and adventure." School chapel meetings during part of the war were held in the Hall behind Worthing Tabernacle, and Leslie Land's evening talks at chapel were "memorable."

In the Summer Term of 1944 Leslie Land wrote a Headmaster's Letter to the school:

> I find it difficult to believe that this is my last term as Headmaster of Seaford College. Many of you are aware that for some time past I felt more and more called to a full time Christian Ministry. About a month ago a way opened unexpectedly. I was offered a post-graduate scholarship at Mansfield College, Oxford, for further theological studies in preparation for the Baptist Ministry; about the same time I was accepted by the authorities of the Baptist Union as a candidate for the ministry following such a course at Oxford. Mrs Land and I believe that this is God's way for us.

The development of this conviction is portrayed in the next chapter. He gained a subsequent BLitt from Mansfield College,

---

[7] These memories are from documents in the archive of the Leicester and Leicestershire Records Office.

Oxford University, writing a comprehensive dissertation (he had read almost 150 books) on 'The Influence of the Victorian Home on the Religious Development of the Child in the Last Three Decades of the Nineteenth Century.' A friend recalls Leslie Land's anecdote about the end of his time at Mansfield:

> As an evangelical he was the odd one out. They were all 20-year-olds and he was probably 40-years-old ... It was a habit for them to ask one of the students to preach the service at the end (of the university year), so ... they asked him to preach, and he said "I preached an evangelical sermon and the principal came up to me afterwards. He said 'Well Land, I see we haven't taught you anything!'" So Leslie said "Oh, but you have. After three years here you've convinced me that all I ever believed was the real gospel."[8]

At some point he took on the pastorate of Bognor Regis Baptist Church,[9] and first spoke at Melbourne Hall in July 1946, returning on October 6. By December the invitation had been offered to him. After a few weeks thought he eventually wrote saying he was "delighted to accept the call" after "much prayerful waiting upon God."

He arrived in Leicester with his wife Kathryn and their young son Peter. His induction took place on May 29th 1947, with Lloyd-Jones as the preacher. His brief years at Melbourne Hall from 1947 to 1961 were significant far beyond the realization of many people at the time. He was there following a time when

---

[8] The principal was Nathanael Micklem, a British theologian and political activist. He surfaced in the correspondence between Leslie Land and Martyn Lloyd-Jones.

[9] Bognor Regis is a town and seaside resort in West Sussex on the south coast of England, 55.5 miles (89 km) south-west of London. The Baptist church is now Opengate Church. According to their records he was minister from some time in 1945 until he left in 1947.

a combination of contemporary, expository, experiential and doctrinal preaching had become largely unknown. F. B. Meyer had been Melbourne Hall's first minister in the late 19th century. W. Y. Fullerton and Benjamin Gibbon were names of subsequent ministers who had long ministries and shaped the church. However, by the end of Gibbon's long ministry that immediately preceded Leslie Land it had become, in the memory of someone there at the time of his arrival, a rather 'social church.' Leslie Land avoided labels, but his gentle, impeccably courteous, yet penetrating expositions laid the foundations of a Reformed evangelicalism which was to influence many beyond his own congregation. By way of just one illustration, 99 people were baptized by him in the three years from October 1947, and 111 joined the church.[10] Christians, ministers included, travelled from all over the city and county to attend his weekly Bible School. His Bible teaching was associated with a great missionary vision, which is sketched in Chapter Six.

We will encounter him through his ministry as a person, pastor and preacher, in the following chapters, but in his resignation letter to the church on November 25, 1961, he reminded them "I have not shrunk from passing on to you the whole counsel of God. I have sought to emphasise none other loyalty than Christ and His Word."

---

[10] The baptism and membership figures do, of course, overlap.

Leslie Land

W. Leslie Land

He realised he had not been able to bring everyone with him in the strong evangelical position he had maintained, yet in a final letter to the church on 27 December 1961 he remarked looking back that "God has sought and saved many souls (I must have baptised several hundred)." He expressed his disappointment that he would be unable to take the weddings of the young people in the church. The impact of his ministry on young people had always been close to his heart and strikingly evident over the years. To the end he was envisioning large things for the church. We will see later how a notice in the December 1961 magazine announced that "Rev. Dr. James Packer of Oxford" was to be the speaker at a meeting of a Lay Preachers Fellowship that month.

Though I was a teenage Christian of only eighteen months standing when he left Melbourne Hall, I retain memories of sermons as clearly now as if I had heard them in recent months. It was not until I arrived at university and was faced with all the debates and decisions that challenge Christian Unions and undergraduates that I began to appreciate the extent to which I had unwittingly been shaped and strengthened by his ministry.

The frequent recommendations of good books, including the latest publications of the infant *Banner of Truth Trust*, tucked away in the pages of his monthly magazine and on the church bookstall, and the string of good preachers occupying his pulpit whenever he was away, were alike testimony to his quiet determination.[11]

The story is told of a later minister of Melbourne Hall being persuaded by his future wife to go with her to Westminster Chapel in London on an occasion when Land was in the pulpit.

---

[11] More is said about his reading and wider networks in Chapter Six.

The experience led directly to Paul Bassett becoming a Christian, and he always recalled Land's "quite remarkable" prayer and the message on being born again. No doubt that day he knelt in prayer before commencing his message, in his flowing black academic gown, as he did without fail in his own church. Doubtless also he leaned his elbows on the pulpit as he urged trusting faith on his hearers with characteristic quiet, almost intimate, insistence.

In 1996 a minister, then living in South Wales, reached retirement. He wanted to find a home for a box of large reel to reel tapes which had been stored away for some years. By a roundabout route Vernon Salkeld passed them on to me. Such is the occasional serendipity of the Christian life! The box was full of mid-week "Bible School" messages by Land given in the closing years of his time at Melbourne Hall.[12] Two of his studies from this period on the second coming of Jesus appear in this book. His account of his motive will stand more generally for his overall preaching ministry.

> I am writing to those who want to come with a fresh love and simple faith to the word of God. They do not know all this intricate prophetical detail, this labyrinthine, pigeon-hole detail which has divided even believers. And I am not sorry that some of them do not know it!

There is a constant modesty in his biblical interpretation, always ready to acknowledge when he did not understand. Yet he does not duck difficult questions. His was no lowest common denominator breed of evangelicalism. Wearing his scholarship lightly, his writing "floats like a butterfly, stings like a

---

[12] For a series of six studies on the final appearing of Jesus see W. Leslie Land, *The Appearing of Jesus*, ed. Ian Shaw (Ian Shaw, 2014).

bee." Reading the chapters in the second part of this book is a salutary experience—chastening yet encouraging. He left Melbourne Hall in December 1961, perhaps underestimating the influence of his ministry. In chapter six, we will see his remark in a farewell letter to the church that "It would be foolish to imagine that *everyone* in so large a fellowship is 'with me' in the strong evangelical position I have sought to maintain." He once remarked, "Oh, how I know it is not easy or even pleasant to have to say these things, and it does not make for popularity: but the days are perilous, and the time is short. Faithfulness, not popularity, will count in the Day of Christ."[13]

He insisted at the close of a Bible School message towards the end of his ministry,

> I am going to preach grace while He lends me breath, and I am going to invite sinners whether they are Jews or Gentiles to put their trust in Jesus. You can trust him now. If Jesus comes tonight, at midnight, or in the morning, you will be with him for eternity.

His wish would not have changed one jot from the prayer that closed his studies on the final appearing of Jesus.

> We thank you Lord for saving us. We thank you for warning us and telling us what to expect. Now come to our hearts afresh. May we be found among those who love your appearing and are ever on our Father's business. Send us out with a holy desire to live more for the things that matter, and to expend less thought and energy on the things that are rapidly passing away. So shed abroad your love in our hearts that we might be able to breathe this prayer, and dare to say, "Even so, come Lord

---

[13] From a sermon on James 3:6, preached at the beginning of 1960.

Jesus! Come and cleanse us. Come and sanctify us. Come and make us whole, that we might be ready for you to come." For Jesus' sake. Amen.

Editor's Note

Throughout this book the structure of the original studies is unchanged. Leslie Land's argument needed no improving. Despite the obvious pastoral intent of all he said and wrote, his style was spare and clear, and marked by a frequent dry humour. He was, of course, primarily, almost solely, concerned with the spoken rather than the written word. He never, as far as I know, considered turning his studies into books. He was speaking to the present not for the eye of posterity. I have felt free to edit, very lightly, his English to retain the immediacy he aimed for. He used the Authorised/King James Version. In general, I have taken the liberty of transposing this into the English Standard Version, except in those various cases where the context demands respect for the original. He frequently translated or paraphrased the text, and I have not interfered with his quotations when his intention was apparently to make the sense clearer or more idiomatic.

Chapter 2
Martyn Lloyd Jones and Leslie Land:
A Christian Friendship

> "I have never known anyone with whom I have felt a closer sense of kinship and true fellowship than yourself." (Lloyd-Jones to Land. September 2, 1942)

> "Among the many with whom I come in contact so regularly there is none with whom (I have) such real affinity." (Lloyd-Jones to Land. July 14, 1943)

The Bible has much to say about Christian friendship, by way of both reflection and example. Christian lifestyle websites, offering friendship, proliferate, and with the advent of the social media the word "friend" increasingly calls for inverted commas. Yet the deepest friendships, perhaps by their very nature, often remain hidden from view. The relationship between Martyn Lloyd-Jones and Leslie Land provides a telling instance of such an unknown and out of sight friendship. For a period of more than twenty years in the middle of the last century, two men—one whose ministry is rightly renowned, the other whose ministry and life are unjustly forgotten—enjoyed a friendship and fellowship that was close to the heart of their lives over that period. We know from the biographies[1] that Lloyd-Jones nurtured a number of rich relationships with

---

[1] Among the various biographical accounts of Martyn Lloyd-Jones' life and ministry, the single volume by Iain H Murray, *The Life of Martyn Lloyd-Jones, 1899-1981.* (Edinburgh: Banner of Truth Trust, 2013), is an excellent introduction.

ministers and others, where he aimed to encourage and establish a strong testimony to the gospel, but as a hidden history this has much on which to remark.

Was Land "unjustly forgotten"? Undeniably so. It was Lloyd-Jones again, in his last surviving letter to Land during a period when the latter was suffering an anxiety-related illness and unable to conduct his ministry, who remarked "I often think of you and pray for you and I have been overjoyed to hear of the great and manifest blessing that has attended your ministry at Leicester" (March 26, 1957).

A Growing Relationship, 1938–1939

Land first approached Lloyd-Jones by letter in late 1938.[2] The timing is significant. It was within weeks of Lloyd-Jones' first service at Westminster Chapel in September that year, following his move from South Wales. New to a church very different from his Sandfields congregation in South Wales, with a young family, the threat of war beginning to loom over the capital, and with no guarantee of his future tenure, Lloyd-Jones was no doubt somewhat alone. We may suspect, given how quick he was off the mark to send the invitation, that Land already knew something of Lloyd-Jones' ministry. When Lloyd-Jones did not immediately reply, we can be thankful he wrote again. "My thanks for your further kind letter. I feel I must respond this time," came the response shortly before Christmas. Land was writing to invite Lloyd-Jones to speak at Seaford College, and he was clearly happy to accept: "I look forward much to the

---

[2] The quotations from letters to Leslie Land from Martyn Lloyd-Jones are from an archive of his letters in the possession of Rev Iain Murray. The relationship between the two men and their families is traced primarily chronologically, but from time to time I have expanded the chapter to show how issues and themes came to hold a larger place in Leslie Land's life and ministry.

pleasure of meeting you." After delaying until March to clarify his diary, he settled to speak on Wednesday, July 13, 1939.

The relationship immediately moved to a closer level. Land seems to have written again the same day of the visit, and on the very next day Lloyd-Jones wrote back in terms that illustrate the warmth and appreciation he felt. Addressing his note to "My dear Land" (instead of the formal "Dear Mr. Land") he remarks in response to something in Land's letter, "You'll see I have obeyed!" but explains that he was unable to provide a copy of his Seaford message for the School magazine because it did not exist. He goes on to say "I cannot tell you how much I enjoyed myself on Wednesday. I was telling Dr. Douglas Johnson of the IVF[3] about it … on the telephone. He will be after you." Douglas Johnson no doubt did go after him, and Leslie Land was to speak often in future years at Inter-Varsity Fellowship national conferences at Swanwick in central England, and at Christian Unions.

The personal and spiritual attraction was clearly mutual. From his summer retreat at Aberystwyth on the coast of West Wales in early August that same year Lloyd-Jones replied to an interesting letter from Land which had "chased me round the country for several days." In an informal tone, Lloyd-Jones tells him that

We are here until Aug 25th and then I go right into the hinterland of Central Wales to preach to a small community of sheep farmers and shepherds. I wish you were

---

[3] For an invaluable account that places Douglas Johnson in the context of the history of British evangelicalism see Oliver Barclay, *Evangelicalism in Britain 1935-1995: A Personal Sketch* (Leicester: Inter-Varsity Press, 1997).

with us! Hope you are all well. I look forward to our next meeting very much.[4]

The subject of Land's letter is of interest. He had clearly been thinking through issues related to evolution, an interest reflected in the final piece included in this book. Lloyd-Jones, away from his library, was obviously caught on the hop and replied, "I cannot quite recall the point to which you refer in Warfield's 'Antiquity of the Human Race' and therefore I will not commit myself to any statement until I have refreshed my memory."[5] Land's position on evolution is included in the final piece by him included in this book.

The early weeks of the Second World War were ones of uncertainty. In October of 1939 Lloyd-Jones told him "At the moment we are carrying on at Westminster with the second service at 3pm instead of 7pm. My family, of course, is evacuated to Wales leaving me here a miserable bachelor-husband."

Conversations about the Ministry, 1940-1941

Land spent several years considering his growing sense of a call to the ministry. In some ways his life echoed that of Lloyd-Jones—just three years in age separated these able and scholarly men whose careers promised and indeed had achieved much, and both called to the uncertainty of Christian ministry. For Leslie Land the years of decision from late 1939 to 1944 directly paralleled the War. They also took place at a period when the revival of spiritual strength in evangelicalism

---

[4] Martyn Lloyd-Jones, Letter to Leslie Land, August 9, 1939.
[5] The reference is to B.B. Warfield's essay "On the Antiquity and the Unity of the Human Race" from *Princeton Theological Review* (1911). Leslie Land was to address issues of science and the Christian faith several times in his subsequent ministry.

associated with Lloyd-Jones, the Inter-Varsity Fellowship, Ernest Kevan, John Stott, James Packer, Elwyn Davies, Alan Stibbs and others was but a cloud the size of a man's hand.

He shared his growing convictions with Lloyd-Jones early in 1940, who replied in encouraging terms:

> Many, many thanks for your letter. It is a real privilege to be allowed to share your confidence at such a vital period in your story. That you are being led clearly and definitely is abundantly evident. The only important thing is that you are led to the right place and the right sphere for the start. My own experience at the same juncture was that the guidance there again will be equally definite if you will be patient. I thought I was to go to a certain place and I wanted to go there. But it was not to be. When I went to Port Talbot I knew at once it was *the* place. And so it proved to be.[6]

Land seems to have contemplated joining his brother Eric Land in his ministry at Worthing, but in reply to further information from Land, Lloyd-Jones says, "I feel that I must see you as I am not happy about you considering your brother's church." The reasons for this are not clear, and indeed, the question of Land's possible links to his brother's church continued to unsettle both Land and Lloyd-Jones for several years. Three months later Lloyd-Jones was tentatively advising "I feel inclined to say that if the door is still open at your brother's church at [Worthing] that you should accept it," but later letters suggest this was never straightforward. They met in London on May 9, 1940, and this was immediately followed by successful efforts on Lloyd-Jones' part to arrange a meeting

---

[6] Martyn Lloyd-Jones, Letter to Leslie Land, April 9, 1940.

between Land and Melbourn Aubrey, then General Secretary of the Baptist Union, which took place on May 15.[7]

Lloyd-Jones' initial reaction to that meeting was positive, and when Land apparently expressed doubts, he assured him: "I regard Aubrey's letter as being eminently satisfactory! For a man who has spent his last fifteen years in writing and preparing diplomatic and non-committal statements I think it is really good."

He again urged patience. Referring to his own decision to leave medicine for the ministry in 1926 without any settled future, he says 'I will understand how you feel. I was exactly the same fourteen years ago and, at times, almost despaired. But all worked out in the right way. My counsel to you therefore is 'Let patience have her perfect work.'"[8]

But nothing was to come of this. The wartime impact on south of England churches was economic as much as spiritual and depleted congregations often were not in a position to meet the financial needs of ministers. The Baptist Union people may also have been wary of the strong evangelicalism of Land and Lloyd-Jones, and the latter continued to explore opportunities for Land, although without success. His own future was deeply uncertain for partly similar reasons. Of the Westminster Chapel congregation, he confides to Land in ways that show how their relationship had quickly moved to a place where Lloyd-Jones wished and felt able to share sensitive information with him.

---

[7] Aubrey had other coincidental associations with Land. His first church had been Victoria Road Leicester—F.B. Meyer's church prior to him moving to Melbourne Hall—and he had also been a scholar at Mansfield College.

[8] Martyn Lloyd-Jones, Letter to Leslie Land, May 12, 1940.

Martyn Lloyd-Jones

We moved to the Livingstone Hall because a number of people, including Dr Morgan, has become somewhat scared. But it has not been a success and we shall soon be returning to the church. I say "we" but the whole question of my future is in the melting pot. As we are going on at the moment it is clear that the church cannot continue to support two ministers. We are about £15 to £20 down each Sunday and we are living on a reserve fund collected last year. Dr Morgan has to go on and cannot retire because he is penniless. He has been most improvident and indeed prodigal. At his age and in his infirmity he cannot go elsewhere. That means that I shall probably go. I offered to do so at the end of September. They would not hear of it then but it seems to me to be quite inevitable.[9]

The same letter has fascination for other reasons. Land had obviously posed the idea to Lloyd-Jones that he might consider applying to the Church of England. This had clearly been the subject of conversation with them already and Lloyd-Jones' reply is interesting for the light it sheds on the thinking of both men at this period:

> Your letter is most interesting. As regards the Church of England I think I mentioned the possibility to you in one of our chats. As far as I am concerned there is nothing whatsoever against it. Indeed, I am not at all sure but that in many ways it would be the right thing for you. I am persuaded that Nonconformity is going to have a real fight for existence after this war. It seems to be the case, in England especially, that the Church has a better opportunity. However, you will be led. The matter of a brief training will not worry you. Again, I believe there is

---

[9] Martyn Lloyd-Jones, Letter to Leslie Land, November 25, 1940.

much to be said in favour of that especially at a place such as the BCMS Bristol.[10] Please do let me know what happens.[11]

By the end of 1941 the Baptist Union avenue seemed to have closed. Land had been rebuffed once more when, in a hard to decipher letter, Lloyd-Jones suggests, "There is but one explanation—their courage finally failed them. And they are probably over-influenced by Aubrey and perhaps Wilkinson Riddle."[12] The sound of closing doors can perhaps be heard:

> However, as you say, it is perfectly clear that it was not God's will that you should go there. And it is certain that He has something better in store for you. I have had such experiences and I can testify absolutely that when one is content to rest in Him everything works out for the best. "Let patience have her perfect work" must be your text once more.[13]

Writers and a Resolution at Last, 1942–1945

Their friendship, however, was to continue and deepen. Three months after the previous exchange, Land appears to have sent Lloyd-Jones an article he had written. Their correspondence on this and other writers in the following months shows both an exchange of minds and a remarkable bond. In reply in

---

[10] There is a valuable account of theological training at Bristol a few years later in Alistair McGrath, *To Know and Serve God: a Life of James I Packer* (London: Hodder and Stoughton, 1997).

[11] Martyn Lloyd-Jones, Letter to Leslie Land, November 14, 1941.

[12] T. Wilkinson Riddle was the popular minister of George Street Baptist Church, Plymouth, and author of *The Faith of a Christian Mystic, The Quest for Truth, For Flag and Empire* and other books. He was happy to be known as someone who would "follow the gleam that leads to the Truth" (Dust jacket of *The Quest for Truth*).

[13] Martyn Lloyd-Jones, Letter to Leslie Land, November 14, 1941.

February 1942, Lloyd-Jones expresses appreciation and encouragement.

> This address of yours is very good. I am so glad to have an opportunity of reading something written by you at last. Quite apart from the matter, your style appeals to me very much. You ... have a literary gift. And you must encourage and develop it. Various things cause me to think of you quite frequently and to wonder how you are.[14]

Lloyd-Jones' judgement was to the point, but for reasons not altogether clear Land wrote nothing for publication.

We encountered Warfield early in their correspondence. He is joined by others. Lloyd-Jones found time to listen to the radio on Sundays. He found time to recommend—and to mention the price! "I wonder if you have been listening on the wireless on Sundays recently to C S Lewis. He is really good. Have you read his 'Problem of Pain'? It is first rate. It is in the Christian Challenge Series 3/6."[15]

Land was later to make sure that books by C.S. Lewis were in the Melbourne Hall library. Later that same year he sent Lloyd-Jones a gift of a book. It was almost certainly the first volume of Karl Niebuhr's *The Nature and Destiny of Man*. Writing back on September 2, 1942, Lloyd-Jones' cannot hide the warmth of his response"

> My dear Land,
> On Saturday afternoon the parcel arrived and left me just speechless. I really do not know how to thank you. And yet you should not have done it. You know from our conversation the other day what I think of the book and

---

[14] Martyn Lloyd-Jones, Letter to Leslie Land, February 1942.
[15] Martyn Lloyd-Jones, Letter to Leslie Land, February 1942.

how anxious I was to possess it in order that I may go through it thoroughly again. But your inscription inside makes it still more precious to me.

It was this gift that prompted one of the sentences that stands as an epigraph to this chapter: "I have never known anyone with whom I have felt a closer sense of kinship and true fellowship than yourself." He adds "And I still feel confident that the future has much in store for us together."

The work at Westminster Chapel was beginning to show signs of blessing. Writing the following April, Lloyd-Jones tells Land,

> You will be glad to hear also that our congregations at Westminster have been slowly but definitely increasing in size. And in addition to that many have remarked on the intense listening. The main task here is to turn an intellectual listening into a vital one. You will know what I mean by that.

He goes on to explain:

> More and more am I being drawn to see that the greatest need today is the power of the Holy Spirit in and through individuals. Right theology is essential but without the power given by the Spirit it can achieve nothing. So many say that theology therefore matters nothing. I reply— "You cannot have a true and valuable fire without first setting the paper and the wood and the coal. A fire made of shavings soon gives out."[16]

---

[16] Martyn Lloyd-Jones, Letter to Leslie Land, April 17, 1943.

He was meeting with Lloyd-Jones for discussion and fellowship. The correspondence contains numerous hints and echoes of a rich relationship. Lloyd-Jones' family members recall Leslie and Kathryn staying at the family home. They both delved into and exchanged thoughts about the literature of the time. Lloyd-Jones continues in the same letter,

> I agree entirely with what you say about Niebuhr. Like so many of these men he has undergone a philosophical conversion. They are all right until they come to the Bible. Philosophically I still find that Niebuhr's book is one of the best for many years. We shall be able to see more exactly where he is when vol. 2 appears. But I am not too hopeful.

He comments on others, for example, the Congregationalist and ecumenical leader Nathanael Micklem:

> If you have Micklem's Lent book in mind, I was frankly disappointed with it. He allows his doctrine to be determined by his sentiment and seems to me constantly to give the whole case away. He is the victim of his own geniality. I fear he is an essayist rather than a theologian.[17]

The second volume of Niebuhr came out some months later and Land bought it for Lloyd-Jones. "I do not know how to thank you both for your letter and the second volume of Niebuhr's Gifford lectures" replied Lloyd-Jones in July 1943:

---

[17] This letter is printed in full in Murray, *D. Martyn Lloyd-Jones. Letters 1919-1981,* 66–67, and repays careful reading for the light it sheds on Lloyd-Jones' range of reading and thinking.

What you have inscribed in that book touches me very deeply indeed and I treasure your words more than I can tell you. I can say quite honestly and frankly that one of the greatest pleasures in life to which I look forward to these days is to meet you.[18]

It is on this occasion that he says "Among the many with whom I come in contact so regularly there is none with whom (I have) such real affinity," adding "My one regret is that we cannot see each other more frequently." It may have been the case that Lloyd-Jones had little fellowship with other ministers in London and was, at least for a time, rather isolated.

It was at this time that Land was taking steps to equip himself further for the ministry. The details are not entirely clear. While we know that the Mansfield College post-graduate scholarship was offered for the 1944–1945 academic year, for reasons somewhat obscure there seems to have been some opposition to the steps he had taken, which would not have been easy. In October of 1943 Lloyd-Jones replied to a further letter with "many many thanks." "I cannot tell you how grieved I was to read its contents. How busy the devil is! The fact that you wrote as you did makes me feel still more closely attached to you. There is much I could say but I will refrain …"[19] He was to stay with Leslie and Kathryn at some point in the following weeks. In an undated letter but written from his new home in Ealing to which he moved in November 1943, Lloyd-Jones says, perhaps tongue in cheek, "I regard myself as a terrible fellow in landing myself on you on Wednesday night. But it is always such a joy to see you … that I felt I could not resist it." He added "I fear you must meet me at the station as I am not

---

[18] Martyn Lloyd-Jones, Letter to Leslie Land, July 14, 1943.
[19] Martyn Lloyd-Jones, Letter to Leslie Land, October 10, 1943.

quite certain of getting to your home and especially in the blackout. It is really good of Mrs. Land to have me. She knows that my tastes are very simple."[20]

By the summer of 1944 the path to the scholarship became clear. 'I am overjoyed at the news contained in your letter of this morning. It is wonderful. I can now see quite clearly the meaning of all the delays and ... disappointments. God's way is always perfect. You have been wonderfully patient and your patient attitude is now going to be rewarded richly."[21] The nature of this occasion is perhaps authentically recalled in the following account given later to a friend by Leslie Land, regarding how the scholarship came about:

> I rang Lloyd-Jones back again, (and) said "I've got this interview ... with Payne." "Oh," he said, "I'll come with you!" Imagine, going to an interview and taking Lloyd-Jones with you! So Leslie said ... "Actually what happened was Lloyd-Jones interviewed Payne, then said 'We'll take it!' ... No, Payne didn't interview us, Lloyd-Jones interviewed Payne!"[22]

Land was probably a "glass half empty" person, and in March 1945, in the months when Lloyd-Jones was himself being tried following bomb damage to Westminster Chapel, we find him again encouraging Land to persevere with the Oxford course: "I am not at all surprised about what you say re Oxford.

---

[20] This is from an undated letter, but written from an address in Ealing, London, where Lloyd-Jones was living from November 16, 1943.

[21] June 4, 1944.

[22] If this memory is correct the Ernest Payne referred to was a British Baptist administrator and scholar. He served the Baptist Union as a pastor, teacher and writer before becoming its general secretary and president. A dedicated ecumenist, he held high office in the Free Churches, the British Council of Churches and the World Council of Churches, where he was elected president

But I think you must stay the second year. It will all help you and add to your ministry in the end. And in the meantime you are doing good work."[23]

Continuing Threads, 1945 Onwards

It proved understandably less feasible for Land and Lloyd-Jones to meet so often in the years that followed. We know as much when Lloyd-Jones tells Land,

> It has been a great source of grief to me that our busy lives have prevented our seeing one another as frequently as I should like. But I often think of you and pray for you and I have been overjoyed to hear of the great and manifest blessing that has attended your ministry at Leicester.

He began his ministry on May 18, 1947 and his induction, as mentioned earlier, was on May 29. In a gesture that would have moved Land deeply, Lloyd-Jones was the preacher, and he, together with Leslie Land, spoke again at an evening public meeting. Lloyd-Jones spoke in the afternoon on the nature of the Christian church, based on the life of Gideon. At the evening meeting he paid a personal tribute to Land, "speaking of his great and varied gifts." The church magazine briefly records it as follows:

> Dr Jones (*sic*) reminded us of the true mission of the Christian church—to ensure that amid the Babel of voices falling on modern ears, the voice of God, the word of the Lord, was most surely heard. Our chief business was to hold forth the "Word of God, which lives and abides for ever."[24]

---

[23] Martyn Lloyd-Jones, Letter to Leslie Land, March 5, 1945.
[24] Melbourne Hall Magazine, July 1947.

The story shades into the account in the following chapters of Leslie Land's ministry at Melbourne Hall. But relevant to the present thread it is known that Land went through at least two lengthy periods when he had to stand back from his ministry due to anxiety and perhaps depression. In March 1957 Lloyd-Jones sent a long letter to him—one of the few that was not initiated by Leslie Land.[25] "I cannot tell how sorry I was to hear from one of your members who happened to be visiting London that you were not well. I gather that it is entirely due to over-work, and, knowing you, I am not at all surprised." "Knowing you" is an apparent reference to his disposition.[26] Land's sadness of mind opens an insight into Lloyd-Jones' typical counsel on such topics, and it merits a relatively full extract:

> 1. Your present trouble is only temporary. It is quite a common happening at your age and it will in no way affect you permanently it is quite a common experience and one from which the patient invariably makes a full recovery. Do not analyse your symptoms. Still less be worried about them. Our nervous system can play all sorts of tricks with us and if we begin to consider each symptom we can become very worried. Avoid that. Just relax completely and give nature a chance.
>
> 2. Don't be in too much of a hurry. Reconcile yourself to the fact that for the time being you must do just nothing. That is the way to prepare for the future.
>
> 3. Do not think at all about the work at Leicester. It is God's, not yours, and he will care for it.

---

[25] This remarkably helpful letter is printed in full in Murray, *D. Martyn Lloyd-Jones. Letters 1919-1981.*

[26] Brian Beardsworth, a retired GP and friend of both Land and Lloyd-Jones, confirmed this extensively from his personal memories.

4. You will find that this experience will be most re-
warding spiritually. It will bring you as it has brought me
to rest more in the love and perfect wisdom of God. I am
sure that He has something special for you in all this for
which you will thank Him all your life. It will enrich your
ministry.

Rest in him and abandon yourself entirely to him.[27]

The final words in this long correspondence are poignant.
"Your people at Leicester who love you so dearly and value
your ministry so highly are praying for you and your many
friends elsewhere, among whom I am happy to count myself,
are doing likewise." We have referred to the letters Land wrote
to his church when he ended his ministry at Melbourne Hall in
December 1961. We know that he preached at Westminster
Chapel several times during the summers in the 1950s.[28] Although Melbourne Hall cannot track down a record for this, a
friend recalls an occasion around 1960 when Land succeeded
in inviting Lloyd-Jones to speak at Melbourne Hall, probably
to the Bible School. Leslie Land

> came into the pulpit, with the Doctor behind him, and he
> hadn't got his gown, he'd got an ordinary suit on. I'd
> never seen him with a suit on before, but I do remember
> this, he just came into the pulpit, said "Let us pray", and
> I can remember, it was an inspiring prayer. So much so
> … he … gripped the whole meeting.[29]

His public prayer was indeed notable. The same friend again
who recalls "I can remember his prayers, they were so natural

---

[27] Murray, 1994. Letter of March 26, 1957.
[28] Margaret Manton notes that he preached there in 1956, 1957, and 1958. Westminster Chapel is unable to confirm these dates.
[29] Brian Beardsworth, Interview with the author, March 17, 2012.

and unaffected, they were unministerial prayers." The prayer that closed Chapter One is a case in point. We have seen how, in the providence of God, the relationship between Lloyd-Jones and Leslie Land led to a subsequent connection through the conversion of Paul Bassett.

In the following chapters Leslie Land appears to us as a person, a pastor and a preacher.

Chapter 3
A Leicester Awakening

We have traced how Leslie Land had risen to become Head of
Seaford College, an independent school in Sussex, before grad-
ually coming to terms with a call to the ministry, and how his
long correspondence and friendship with Martyn Lloyd-Jones
played a central role in him leaving his position and moving,
via a scholarship to Mansfield College (Oxford) and a short
ministry on the south coast of England, to Melbourne Hall in
the East Midlands city of Leicester in 1947.[1]

The Times and the Church

1947—in some ways so recent, in others so distant. The Second
World War had its ever-present legacies for the members of
Land's new church. A Forces "Welcome Home" meeting took
place in the September shortly following his arrival. There is a
note of the British and Foreign Bible Society calling for German bibles.[2] In the following month he has a note about a letter he had given the church for funds for bombed churches and
the result was to that date £243 (a substantial sum) had been
donated. There was also a note in the December issue of the
church magazine about a planned plaque for those from the
church who died during the war and a provisional list of twelve
names is given. When the plaque was unveiled he preached on
"What causes wars?" "War has its origin in the human soul."

---

[1] The sources for this are bound copies of the substantial monthly church magazine, plus correspondence, audiotape transcripts, and other archival sources. I cite details of dates and sources only where the context calls for them.

[2] Now simply The Bible Society

Leaders of some fanatical party may be an immediate cause but they "are like an eruption on the crust of a diseased world."

Melbourne Hall, Leicester

National fears lingered. Reflecting his constant interest in science and the Christian faith, he spoke often of the possibility of atomic warfare. He was both biblical and contemporary when he wrote in October 1947, two years after Hiroshima, on "The Mighty Atom." Asking why people were fearful he suggests, "It is not the *atom* they really fear. It is not science. It is these things in the hand of *man* they fear ... Our silent tears and misgivings are a striking testimony to the verdict of God's Word about Man: That he is away from his Lord and Maker."[3] He reflected, "There is something of the awful nemesis of Romans 1 about it all ... What it may mean in *our* day if God gives up men to go their own way we can only faintly imagine."

But he never simply bemoans. He speaks of "the design of the atom. So complex—and yet so perfect." He speaks of the atom as a kind of microcosm of the universe in its perfection and design. Yet the scientist has found a way of breaking up the atom and "letting loose those vast stores of energy in wild confusion. The order, the harmony is destroyed and the very matter is disintegrated and lost" and adds "What a picture of the plight of man!" Returning to the theme a year later, his stance is always that "man out of his own resources can find no hiding place from the tragic and inexorable consequences of his sin and shame," such that through atomic fission even "the material universe is crying out ... 'No place to hide.'" He concludes how in the Gospel "there *is* a place to hide, there is One Hiding Place for man," and that "The Saviour's Cross is the nucleus and the centre of a new creation."[4]

What kind of church did Leslie Land arrive at with his wife Kathryn and their young son Peter in May 1947? Big names, as we have seen, had held tenure in the pulpit: F.B. Meyer, W.Y. Fullerton[5] and Benjamin Gibbon. But all was not well. Indeed, even the ministry of Meyer was different in tone from Land.

---

[3] This quotation and the following are from *The Melbourne Hall Magazine* (October 1947): 4–6.

[4] "No Place to Hide," *Melbourne Hall Magazine* (November 1948): 106.

[5] Fullerton (1857–1932) is perhaps best known today for his hymn "I Cannot Tell." He was influenced by Spurgeon in his younger days and wrote extensively.

Meyer had distanced himself from Spurgeon in the Downgrade Controversy.[6] Notwithstanding his appreciation of Spurgeon, Fullerton's preaching was less fitted to ground his hearers in the word of God. For example, he opened one of his sermons, preached on an early November Sunday, with

> Yesterday morning I cast about me to see what subject I should speak upon this evening, and as I thought, fresh gusts of wind carried up the leaves against my window. As I looked at the fallen leaves, there would come to me one word from God's own book that could not be got rid of, and so persistent was it, that I saw no escape; it came again and again, "We all do fade as a leaf."[7]

When Leslie Land arrived, Freemasonry was present within the church. Without confronting the issue head on, he preached and expounded his way, until some years later force of circumstances made a decision on the question of the church's attitude to freemasonry essential. The vote among a very large group of church officers was almost unanimously against membership of secret societies. The anecdote is illuminating, as is the fact that he told this story in 1962 to a small group of schoolboys who turned up unannounced to visit him some months after he had left the church.

Leslie Land, the Person

The person, the ministry, the preaching—all are intertwined. His reading was extensive, though he never wore his

---

[6] Holman (2007) has written an illuminating, if perhaps unduly appreciative, account of Meyer's life, which demonstrates his desire to be fully involved in the broad church of nonconformity.

[7] W.Y. Fullerton, "As a Leaf" (Sermon delivered November 4, 1894), *Melbourne Hall Magazine* (October 1900): 1.

knowledge on his sleeve. A scan of the magazine includes Hudson Taylor, Thomas Huxley, Emil Brunner, John Ruskin, Francis Dixon, David Tryon, J. Oswald Saunders, Oswald Chambers, Ole Hallesby, Charles Spurgeon and extended extracts from Alan Stibbs. The frequent recommendations of good books, including in years to come the latest publications of the infant Banner of Truth Trust, tucked away in the pages of his monthly magazine and on the church bookstall, and the string of good preachers occupying his pulpit whenever he was away, were alike testimony to his quiet determination.[8]

He never lost his early interest in the sciences. His handling of evolution, for example, has continuing value today. Writing in 1949 on "The Christian and the Theory of Evolution" he helpfully resets the discussion, such that the question becomes "How can we account for the world and life, leaving God and His creative acts out of the reckoning?" He is not an obscurantist and speaks "as a Christian who can claim to have studied the Natural Sciences."[9] He assumes "that changes and modifications may and do take place in the structures of plants and other living organisms no-one would wish to deny" and he seems quite happy to call this "evolution" (though he insists that this is typically a process of simplification not growing complexity). "If by 'Evolution' you mean *this* process that is going on inside, as it were, the family circles of the different kinds of created life, then we agree there *is* such a process; the fossils prove it." He also warns that the bible is not a textbook of science "and should never be misused as such." "But it has a knack of saying profound things in a very simple way."

---

[8] See Chapter Six for a fuller account of Leslie Land's reading.
[9] This and the following linked quotations are from *Melbourne Hall Magazine* (February 1949): 129–131.

Yet he saves the main force of his response for where he started—the assumptions and premises involved:

> The Evolutionary Hypothesis in its full implications has no God in it (and what is worse no gospel). It has a false gospel and a false light in it. It leads man to suppose that his feet are on an evolutionary ladder, that he is climbing higher and higher, and getting better and better. Such an outlook ... can only lead men to disillusionment and despair.

Speaking a year later on the Christian and this present world he says of humanity,

> His conquest of nature, his mastery of science and technology have seemed to bring a wild dream near to the point of realisation. But – Hiroshima! Something has gone wrong ... It is the story of Babel all over again ... Whenever men set themselves to build Utopia, the result always turns out to be a hell.[10]

He pointedly says of the church that "She has compromised her position, offering men her services as an advisor and abettor in this God-shy, Christ-rejecting enterprise."

There is a weaving together of light and darkness in his thought. Speaking on "Moses my servant is dead: now therefore arise, go over this Jordan," he says "Yes—God's servants pass on ... Lament and sorrow? No! 'Arise – go over this Jordan, thou and all this people.' The darker the hour, the grander,

---

[10] This and the following quotation are from the *Melbourne Hall Magazine* (February 1950): 226.

more clarion-like the call."[11] Referring to the uncertainties of possible war,[12] and applying his thought as he often did to young people, he says:

> I don't know what all you young folk are going to do in life … *Here* is something certain! Something tough, but glorious and triumphant. Something to bite on—something to build on—a call to young Joshuas—a call to the service of the King of Kings, the Lord of Lords—a call to leadership for Christ and his kingdom. It is a call to war … The days are grievous, but I believe we are on the eve of great things for God. Yes, amid the confused scene, there is a people waiting to cross over into God's kingdom.[13]

Darkness and Light

Land sometimes succumbed to the pressures his own work regime caused. It is known that he went through at least two lengthy periods when he had to stand back from his ministry due to anxiety and perhaps depression. On one such occasion in March 1957 Lloyd-Jones sent a long letter to him: "I cannot tell how sorry I was to hear from one of your members who happened to be visiting London that you were not well. I gather that it is entirely due to over-work, and, knowing you, I am not at all surprised."[14]

---

[11] This untitled sermon was preached on November 2, 1947, on the occasion of the memorial service for Benjamin Gibbon, the predecessor minister, who died October 27, 1947. *Melbourne Hall Magazine* (December 1947): 19.

[12] The Korean War broke out in June 1950.

[13] In quoting his words I retain the exact way in which he spoke and wrote, without correcting what may seem very occasional infelicities or inconsistencies.

[14] Lloyd-Jones' remarkably helpful letter is printed in full in Iain Murray, *D. Martyn Lloyd-Jones. Letters 1919-1981* (Edinburgh: Banner of Truth Trust, 1994), 76–77.

Scholarly he may have been, but he was a natural communicator. A note in the summer of 1948 about the Sunday School anniversary records how "Mr. Land, having riveted the attention of the children (not to mention adults) by a variety of objects, sights and sounds, led our thoughts, faithfully and very ably, to Christ and His gracious salvation."[15]

His deep seriousness was leavened with a delightful dry humour. There are numerous examples of this, and on a very rare occasion when Leicester City Football Club reached the FA Cup Final, while speaking on giving one's imagination to the message, he says "I listened in not long ago to the Cup Final at Wembley. At one point in the game, I realized I had yielded my imagination to the commentator's story and I was living in it. Believe me or not, I almost scored a goal for Leicester City!"[16]

There is a note that nicely illustrates Land's gentle humour applied to dealing with something that had become a difficulty for him. It begins,

> If you take a stroll in Hyde Park on Sunday afternoon, you will meet two wonderful phenomena – Infants and Orators. If you come to Melbourne Hall on Sunday morning you may experience something similar, except that in this case the Infants are the Orators![17]

He goes on to say, "Now your minister not only has the task of trying to lead the worship, but also that (a much more difficult one) of trying to please a lot of grown-ups!" He suggests to the "dear mothers of Salem" that if their "little ones are showing

---

[15] The note may have been by J.C. Wilcox, the magazine editor and frequent contributor, a grammar school teacher, and without doubt within Land's most valued core of supporters.

[16] Leicester City reached the FA Cup Final in May 1949.

[17] *Melbourne Hall Magazine* (November 1960): 163.

marked vocal talent early on in life," there is a creche to which the service is relayed.

An early message to the centenary meetings of the once well-known temperance movement "The Band of Hope," in October 1947, and included in the opening section of his writing in this book, shows perfectly how he used humour to serve the cause of the gospel, drawing hearers into the humour and then challenging them. He tells how when invited:

> I did my best to decline this invitation and honour conferred on me tonight. I have never signed the "Pledge"! I told him so—but the more I protested the more convinced he seemed to become that the Centenary should be celebrated at Melbourne Hall, myself being the preacher. Let me say here—if signing a pledge helps you, or *would* help you to live a better life, then in God's name sign it my friend.[18]

But he immediately adds "I am one of those who needs something more than a pledge of my own undertaking. The message I bring you tonight concerns that 'something more.'" This message shows his distance from the traditions of the past.[19] He introduces the advertising slogan, "Beer is best" and proceeds:

> You may think I am going to tear ... that slogan ... to shreds—going to expound a few scientific principles—going to recite some physiological consequences, economic consequences—going to add a few harrowing anecdotes and then go away fondly hoping I have made you all total abstainers. I am not going to do anything of the

---

[18]This and the following linked quotations are from the *Melbourne Hall Magazine* (November 1947): 11.

[19] F.B. Meyer had been a strong supporter of the temperance movement.

kind. We will let the slogan stand; for it well placards a certain level or kind of life about which I want to speak plainly tonight.

I am not concerned merely with the "alcoholic"—the poor man or woman in the grip of that awful disease—I am not concerned only with men and women who, otherwise gifted and talented, are sapping and destroying their mental powers and prospects with this accursed habit—I am not thinking only of broken, ruined homes and marriages, or of the crime of cultivating acres for brewing purposes when nations, women and children are perishing for want of wheat and bread. No, I am thinking rather of a level of life which is the best that multitudes of our fellow men and women know—a life roofed in by *this* world—a life which misses the goal and purpose for which Almighty God created men—a life which ends, like the book of Genesis, "in a coffin in Egypt."

Land was eminently a person of prayer. One of the early magazines carries a piece on "The Power of a Praying Church" by Francis Dixon, a minister in Bournemouth, and in January 1949, giving his New Year wishes, he has a New Year Resolution "to pray more in the New Year." He goes on:

It isn't fervour or emotional stress or any spectacular chrism we need to make a prayer meeting real and effective. We haven't come to persuade God concerning something which He is very reluctant to do; we haven't come together to show each other up or to "get one in" at someone; we haven't come to get our own way done in heaven. We have come solely and simply because we want *God's* way done on earth.[20]

He was always ready to be straight with his hearers:

Heaven save us from *long* prayers and from long embarrassing silences ... Oh that we could rid the idea that to take part in a prayer meeting you have to deliver a sermon or evangelical dissertation, or recite the main points of the Bible from Genesis to Revelation.

His response was, "The prayer meeting ... is the Christian's workshop where things are *done* by God and for God... Let us be natural, then, in prayer and very simple. The *supernatural* is with God."

Speaking in June 1950 on revival, and in the context of a Baptist Union call for "advance," he says that their need is for power, and for that we need to "wait for the promise of the Father" rather than proceed by "clever organisation" or "lots of conferences and conventions." "It is so much easier to *organise* than to *agonise*. We will do anything rather than *pray*... The plain truth is we just do not like praying; we find it hard and uninteresting."[21]

His prayerfulness was a foundation of his pastoral commitment. The following chapter takes us further in understanding the extent to which this gives us a continuing pattern.

---

[20] This and the following linked quotations are from "New Year Resolution," *Melbourne Hall Magazine* (January 1949): 123.

[21] "The Wind in the Treetops," *Melbourne Hall Magazine* (June 1950): 258–259.

Chapter 4
A Christian Ministry

When Leslie Land arrived at Melbourne Hall, Leicester in 1947, he probably knew that he would be at odds with some aspects of its established Christian ethos. Having seen that the early post-war years were a time when in the wider Christian world a combination of contemporary, expository, experiential, and doctrinal preaching had become largely unknown, the church officers likely thought they were extending a signal honour to him in inviting him to come to the church. Though it was only after a few weeks thought that he responded to the invitation saying he was "delighted to accept the call' after "much prayerful waiting upon God."[1]

The names and numbers of people either baptised or added to the church membership were listed in the monthly magazine—a weighty product that apparently went into 1000s of homes.[2] He would announce such matters in the following typical way in the pages of the magazine: "There will be a Baptismal Service on Sunday evening, January 30th. If you wish to confess the Saviour please let me know. Informal classes (in my Vestry) will re-open on *Thursday January 13th at 8 pm.*" He did not neglect the spiritual wellbeing of those who had been baptised. For January 1949 there was an announcement. "On New Year Sunday afternoon, the Pastor hopes to meet all those whom he has had the joy of baptizing into Christ since he began his ministry at Melbourne Hall." He planned a tea and fellowship meeting followed by "a simple act of re-dedication to our Lord and Saviour Jesus Christ."

---

[1] *Melbourne Hall Magazine* (February 1947): 225.
[2] *Melbourne Hall Magazine* (October 1947): 1.

On arriving in Leicester, Land may not have been wholly familiar with the writings of the evangelical Calvinists of the East Midlands from 150 years prior to his ministry—William Carey, John Sutcliff, Andrew Fuller, John Ryland and the like. But his ministry was fully in tune with Fuller's belief that the gospel was worthy of, and indeed called for, "full acceptation." Speaking in June 1949 on "Why Isn't Everybody a Christian Believer?" we find one of the occasions when he addresses the doctrines of grace explicitly. It is worth noting for how this shaped his ministry:

> We might approach an answer to this question from two different plains—the earthly and the heavenly: the man-ward side and the God-ward side of the question.
>
> On the manward side it is a matter of our human choice and free will[3] ... On the God-ward side *conversion* ... is a supernatural happening, the impact of the Spirit of God on a human heart. The Bible, without any apology, presents both aspects of a conversion side by side. "No man can come unto Me except the Father draw him," said the Lord Jesus; yet from the same lips we hear the tenderest appeal, "Come unto Me all ye that are weary and are heavy laden and I will give you rest."
>
> The Bible says in effect, "Choose you this day whom you will serve," and yet at the same time, "You have not chosen me; I have chosen you." We must ever seek to hold these great truths of free-will and election in tension—like a stretched piece of elastic ... We do well not to choose the one we think we understand (and therefore like) and neglect the other, but to present *all* the counsel of God and leave the power to Him.[4]

---

[3] Land uses free will to refer to human responsibility. It is clear from his general approach that he does not believe the human will to be "free."

[4] *Melbourne Hall Magazine* (June 1949): 161.

Speaking six months later on "Him that cometh to me," he notes how that before speaking of coming to Him, Jesus has spoken of the Father giving us to Jesus. He talks of the "facet of the Gospel jewel, that the Son of God should so want us that we are, as it were, God's crowning gift to His Son." He continues,

> Here then are two lovely truths side by side. God the Father draws sinners and gives them to His Son; *and* sinners are free to come to Him. No, you cannot reconcile or resolve these two precious truths: just hold them reverently "in tension." Do not let *either* go or you will soon join a sect, specialising in *election* or in *free will*.[5]

His constant concern for the application of the truth is apparent when he goes on to say:

> I am so glad that God *draws* men. It lifts a burden off my mind for *I* could never persuade a man to become a Christian. On the other hand I am delighted that men are free to come to Christ, for that means I may go on inviting them in the name and in the love of Christ.

He applies it evangelistically: "That restlessness, that longing in your soul when you hear the gospel preached is a sign and token that the Father is drawing you to Christ—has *given* you to His Son."

Young People
It would seem that his labours resulted in an almost immediate blessing among the young people who attended, among whom

---

[5] This and the following linked quotations are from the *Melbourne Hall Magazine* (December 1949): 209–210.

were several who would later become active in Christian ministry and witness in Leicester and round the world. His ministry among young people and the encouragement he constantly drew from them is remarkable. By April 1948, a Youth Fellowship Library had been started for "books of a spiritually helpful character," with a committee of Land, J.C. Wilcox, and two young members—John Ward who would later become an elder, and "Miss M. Shuttlewood."[6] By October the following year another of the young people noted that the library "now contains well over one thousand helpful books."[7]

His work with young people seems to have raised a few eyebrows. Hence he has a full note about the Youth Fellowship, because someone in the church had "thought there might be a little misunderstanding about it in a few people's minds."[8] He says that shortly after arriving at Melbourne Hall he had called an open meeting of all young people. Reflecting his concern for a more biblical pattern of the local church he says, "Our aim in view was, and is, to break down any and all the barriers that tend to arise between the various organisations and activities in a church, and to foster Christian FELLOWSHIP." He explains that this had a purpose—a mission—outside as well as inside the church, where people could be introduced. His gentle humour comes through when he says that such an initiative is "not spectacular 'red-hot' evangelistic work. It just calls for steady, prayerful, loyal, consecrated endurance. It is rather like

---

[6] Mary Shuttlewood, later Mary Ward, following her marriage to John Ward mentioned here. He was appointed an elder by Leslie Land at the age of 27 to the apparent misgiving of some. It was through Mary Ward that the bound copies of the church magazine came into my hands.

[7] Note by C[olin] Densham, *Melbourne Hall Magazine* (October 1949): 197.

[8] This quotation and those in the following paragraphs are from the *Melbourne Hall Magazine* (November 1948): 108–109.

gathering rose hips: not very exciting, but they contain Vitamin C!"

The committee mainly comprised young people, and he attended the meetings. It is likely that some were concerned about such a committee, and he stresses it is not a governing body and that any matters concerning church business are always referred via him to the Church Committee, and any matters regarding spiritual aspects are made known via him to the Elders. He concludes by asking their prayer and says that

> It already has the seal of God's blessing upon it. We have a crowd of new faces (at) this new session on Saturday evenings. Please pray that every single one of them may be drawn to the Saviour. *That* is our passion—*that* is our single aim.

In the same issue that announced the launch of the library he included a piece he titled "When Parents Stop Telling." It is an application of the main message of the book of Judges. He notes that at the Exodus the Children of Israel had been told that they should always explain to their children what the Passover meant, and what God had done for them. When a new generation arose that knew not God, it was because parents had stopped telling their children. He urges his readers: "Tell them, that is, not just about the God of the trees, the flowers and the birds, but tell them about a personal, covenant-making, loving and *redeeming* God."[9] He continues to apply his theme by saying that,

---

[9] This and the following quotation are from the *Melbourne Hall Magazine* (April 1948): 52.

The *time in history* at which mothers and fathers stop telling their children the story of God's redemption makes very little difference: the effect, the result is just the same then and now—the same in *kind*, but ever worsening in *degree* as civilization advances with an unsaved soul.

Melbourne Hall Magazine Cover

The responsibilities of parents clearly lay heavily on him. Speaking at the end of 1948 on "What mean ye by this service?" (Ex. 12:26–27), reprinted in this book, he writes about the Lord's Supper, and what we would say if children observed it and asked what it meant, as with the Passover. His points are we should tell our children:

- It is about something that actually happened.
- "We must tell our children a harder thing." It speaks of death—*broken* bread, *outpoured* wine." Not "my body which *lives* for you' but 'my body which is *given* for you." His blood which "is *shed* for you."
- Tell them that he lives, "He is present at the feast." "He is not in the bread," but his presence is like the trust deeds of a house.
- Tell them that God has made a covenant, an agreement, with us: "A lavishly one-sided agreement where God *gives* and we *take*."
- Tell them it is preaching in action: "Ye do *show the Lord's death.*"
- Tell them it is a prophecy. The believer at the Lord's Table may say, "Next time, maybe, at His coming."[10]

We have more to say about his preaching in Chapters Five and Six, but it illustrates his spiritual creativity that he would keep the form of this verse and expound the Lord's Supper as talking to children.

Towards the end of this first three years, he noted that "fourteen young people have expressed their desire to be identified with Jesus Christ as Saviour and Lord" through

---

[10] *Melbourne Hall Magazine* (December 1948):113–115.

baptism.[11] He had held a meeting on New Year's Day, 1950, with all who had been baptized during 1949. "Several young people gave helpful and encouraging words of testimony."[12] Indeed, while sometimes he addresses parents, he often speaks direct to children and young people of all ages. In February 1949 he tells them his encouragement. "My dear young friends, it is a great joy to see so many of you in God's house on Sunday morning." His message we noted earlier on "The Christian and this Present World" (Heb. 11:13–16) closes with this appeal:

> You young people, come on pilgrimage! Take the Lord Jesus Christ as your Saviour, unreservedly and whole-heartedly ... Then go out into the world, living at every point of your character and personality *for Him*. Set out for the Eternal City, ever looking to Jesus; and then, *on the way*, your life will be a benediction and a means of grace to this present sin-sick world.[13]

This urgent concern recurs several times:

> You young Christians, especially—you who have been baptized into Jesus Christ—hazard your lives for Him who laid down His life on Calvary for you and your salvation. Ask God to give you the souls of them that travel with you.

---

[11] This and the following quotations are from the *Melbourne Hall Magazine* (February 1950): 228.

[12] He would record in the February 1956 magazine that on 15 January 1956 six "younger Christians" had given brief words of testimony from the pulpit.

[13] This and the following quotation are from the *Melbourne Hall Magazine* (February 1950): 227.

Bible School

Christians, ministers included, travelled from all over the city and county to attend his weekly Bible School. David Kingdon gave the following anecdote:

> I lived in Leicester for a number of years after Leslie Land finished his ministry in Melbourne Hall. Occasionally I would hear his name mentioned especially by members of the generation who had felt the impact of his remarkable ministry. One day an elder of the Bethel Evangelical Church, Wigston told me a story which illustrates the impact of that ministry on the lives of many of Leslie Land's hearers. It was my friend's custom to attend his weekly Bible School in Melbourne Hall with a group of his friends. More than once such was the sense of awe that came over them that no one spoke in the car as they went home! [14]

An early issue of the magazine carried a Bible School invitation, in which he quotes Hudson Taylor saying, "There is a living God, He has spoken in the Bible. He means what He says and will do all He has promised," and infers from this "there are few greater necessities in our lives than an intelligent understanding of the Word of God."[15] Already he speaks of the Bible School as "proving a tremendous help and blessing to very many within the circle of Melbourne Hall and beyond" and urges the importance of such opportunities in his closing

---

[14] From his Preface to *The Appearing of Jesus*. A brief but incomplete obituary of David Kingdon can be found at www.evangelicalmagazine.com/article/david-p-kingdon and a longer piece, written some years prior to his death, at banneroftruth.org/uk/about/banner-authors/david-p-kongdon. He was the author of a number of valuable books, perhaps especially his *Children of Abraham* (Grace Publications, 2022).

[15] This and the following quotation are from the *Melbourne Hall Magazine* (October 1947): 6.

quotation from Jeremiah 22:29: "O earth, earth, earth, hear the Word of the Lord."

In another note about the Bible School, he says "it was most encouraging ... to see so many young Christians there."[16] He was introducing a *responsive* note leaving aside one week a month in the Bible School to deal with questions and problems about the Christian life, that anyone could post in a box in advance. By the summer of 1948 he is thankful that,

> The very large attendance at our Bible School week by week is most encouraging. The Lord is crowning our mid-week meetings with His blessing: there is an ever increasing love and interest being manifested in the treasures of His word. And what a joy to note that the members of our Youth Fellowship are by no means behind in their keenness on Bible Study.[17]

There is perhaps a hint at the demands of the ministry when he adds: "'Wednesday night at eight' has come to be one of the happiest times of fellowship in Christ along life's difficult way." The first three years of the Bible School were engaged in working through the first fifteen chapters of Romans and by September 1950 he had started a new series on Hebrews.

A Church-Based Ministry

The foregoing makes little sense apart from the realization that Land came to the ministry with a commitment to seeing the whole work of the church as being governed by biblical patterns and principles. He was not reluctant to make the point. Just nine months after he arrived we find him preaching on

---

[16] *Melbourne Hall Magazine* (February 1948): 35.
[17] *Melbourne Hall Magazine* (July 1948): 76.

Hebrews 10:19–25: "not forsaking the assembly of ourselves." He asks why the Hebrew Christians were staying away. In their case he believes it was not indifference but fear: "It cost them a lot to confess Christ."[18] But in 1947, he suggested, such patterns were at root a loss of first love. One can imagine Melbourne Hall perhaps had been marked by long-established forms as part of a big city church, and that some in his congregation may have felt pricked by such implications. But he clearly felt this was a real issue, remarking "as the manner of some (nay, of many) is today." His development is pointed:

> All kinds of secondary reasons might be given. A bit of a cold (too much gardening yesterday): the "so-an-so's" are coming over for the day (you can't give them a cold lunch); some old friends are staying with us – they don't worship anywhere (*very* awkward: one *must* be sociable). Then again, many church members have no intention of going *twice* on a Sunday to God's House. Others say: "We always listen-in to a nice little service on the radio." And so it goes on.[19]

Why does it matter? He goes for the big reasons—rather like his friend and mentor Lloyd-Jones. Noting the context of the passage he says, "This gathering of ourselves together is an inseparable part of a great evangelical, redeeming purpose in the world." His subsequent points are:

- Jesus has opened a way back to God so "we *must* gather together."

---

[18] *Melbourne Hall Magazine* (February 1948): 33.
[19] *Melbourne Hall Magazine* (February 1948): 33.

- In gathering we affirm "our great and holy faith, a faith which is greater and more sure than all the world's habits of thought and chatter."
- "Let is consider one another…" "One another… we are travelling home together … each for the other and for the whole Body of Christ."

He was not a partisan non-conformist. He interestingly says,

We need humbly to pray for our many faithful brethren in the State Church … who are sorely plagued and harassed by a movement in that church to lead them—if not to drive them—back again to that sorry pre-reformation state of affairs, with its candles, confessionals and crucifixes.[20]

It seems clear that he had considered entering the Church of England ministry while still at Seaford College and Land had obviously posed the idea to Lloyd-Jones. During his ministry Melbourne Hall held strong links with several prominent Christians who worked with the Anglican communion. These included Christians whose names now largely are sadly forgotten—John Dean who was a major force for good in northern Nigeria, and John Sperry who held a senior position in the Anglican church in northern Canada.

His commitment to the local church was not without early appreciation on the part of young people in the church. For example, by the November of the first year of his ministerial tenure Young Life Campaign[21] members in Melbourne Hall

---

[20] In the sermon "The Foolishness of Preaching" *Melbourne Hall Magazine* (August 1948): 82.

[21] The National Young Life Campaign (NYLC) was—and still is—a national network of Christian youth groups for teens and twenties based in the UK.

had met and "decided unanimously to form a Church Group with a view to 'more actively supporting their own Church and Minister, whilst retaining their interest in local branch activities of NYLC.'"[22]

His esteem for the Lord's Supper was part and parcel of his church-based ministry. After speaking on the verse, "What mean ye by this service?" he returned to the subject in May 1950 on the injunction, "Let a man examine himself."[23] In his characteristic way he builds from a deceptively straightforward account. "I have just returned from a conference of Christian students in Swanwick, Derbyshire." He remarks, "There was a wonderful fellowship and oneness in spirit." He bridges this to how Christians have often been divided over the meaning of the Lord's Supper. His anti-sacramentalism surfaces when he talks of how the service had first developed:

> *someone* had to handle the bread and the cup … A choice would be made; an Elder, esteemed for his life and Christian character, would be asked … This did not give the particular Elder any claim to a special position spiritually; in fact on the next occasion another trusted disciple would be asked to fulfil these duties.

As numbers grew not all could sit round the table. He observes how the danger of a "top table" got introduced; and how the act of breaking the bread "was relegated to *one* chosen Elder;" and again, "in view of our human perverseness, the danger of attributing to this one man some high-priestly office is already lurking at hand … And so we have come a long way from the

---

[22] *Melbourne Hall Magazine* (November 1947): 15.
[23] This and the following quotations are from the *Melbourne Hall Magazine* (May 1950): 249.

57

simplicity of the Upper Room in Jerusalem through the complexity of the Episcopacy to Roman Catholicism."

He then goes on at fuller length to warn of the same dangers among free churches, and of how the Lord's Supper is spoken of as being "dispensed":

> The Lord's Supper is not a *dispensation*, it is a *Communion* ... It is not primarily communion or fellowship with other Christians, for—let it be said reverently—this is not a club-dinner ... No, this is the communion of each redeemed sinner with the Redeemer. ... Is the Table open then? *Yes!*

He was opposed to any check or examination process by the church: "Surely there should be some check, some inquest, some examination? Yes, but not by *you*, not be *me*. 'Let a man examine himself.'"

On yet another occasion he spoke of The Lord's Table from Luke 15:2: "This man receives sinners and eats with them." He started by referring to how there were those Christians in Scotland who were reluctant to come to the Lord's Table because they did not think themselves fit to do so. While we may be tempted to feel sorry for them, he insists that in one respect they are right:

> They really do sincerely believe and realise that they are coming to meet with Jesus Christ ... The glory, the grace of this feast of memory is the presence of Christ. To gather round the Table is to meet with Him. These Highland sinners are *right* there, and we need to recapture the sense of the presence and the holiness of the Lord Jesus Christ.
>
> But our Scottish friends are wrong, sadly wrong, in staying away through a sense of their sinnership, for the simple reason that these Pharisees, all unwittingly, were

perfectly right when they said "This man receives sinners and eats with them."

A Wider Ministry

The Swanwick reference—the venue for the annual conference of the then Inter-Varsity Fellowship—indicates that early in his time at Leicester he was having a wider ministry. This again owed something to Lloyd-Jones, and we have seen how Lloyd-Jones brought Land into contact with Douglas Johnson of the Inter-Varsity Fellowship.

1950 was not the first time he had spoken at Swanwick. In an intriguing note in March 1948, hinting at the demands that already were mounting, Wilcox, the magazine editor, asks prayer for Land in undertaking "those outside engagements he feels constrained to accept."[24] He was due to speak at the IVF Swanwick conference on April 4. The following year he spent two days in May 1949 speaking to students in the Cambridge Inter-Collegiate Christian Union (CICCU). Later that year, in October, he tells his church that in the next "week or two" he has two ministers' fraternals, a Church Anniversary, a Missionary Conference and a student meeting at Nottingham University. There is also a curious note that he was to address a public meeting in The Little Theatre, Dover St., on "Principles of Nature Cure."[25] We say more about his wider ministry in Chapter Six.

In those days before easy air travel, it was noteworthy that his congregation drew in those from other countries. Reflecting on a morning service on January 25, 1948, for example, he records: "In that congregation there were friends from

---

[24] *Melbourne Hall Magazine* (March 1948): 41.
[25] *Melbourne Hall Magazine* (October 1949): 198. There is no record what his friend Lloyd-Jones thought of this venture!

Germany (one-time "enemies"); from Holland; from Sweden; from Yugoslavia; from Latvia,"[26]

Evangelistic Determination

Several times we have felt the evangelistic resolve beneath his words. To illustrate further, in October of the year he arrived he carried an opening piece called "Scandal!!" and commences with the words that this magazine "is going into thousands of homes in Leicester, and to others outside the city and even across the seas."[27] The tone is typical. He writes on what he calls "the most astonishing 'Scandal' that has ever come to light":

> Men and women, it's like this: This world (and that means *you* and *me* and *everybody*) has got away from God—has turned its back on God: and we're in an awful mess. We can't run our own lives; we can't manage our own world—simply because we're *God's* creatures and it's God's world. This *broken relationship* with our Maker is our curse, our undoing; the deep-root cause of all our unrest and misery. Now, God might have left us to go our own perishing way, but He didn't, He followed us! He came down to this runaway world in Jesus Christ and at a place called Calvary the *broken relationship* has been mended.

But he remarks that the New Testament anticipates our unbelief and refers to this message as a scandal, and offence or stumbling block: "Fancy God saving the world through the crucified Man of Sorrows! Sacrifice..! Blood..! Revolting..! Scandalous..!" He appeals: "Have *you* believed it, friend? Have

---

[26] *Melbourne Hall Magazine* (February 1948): 35.
[27] This and the following quotations are from the very first brief article he wrote for the *Melbourne Hall Magazine* (October 1947): 1.

you tried God's way yet? ... Oh men and women, you'll let me speak plainly to your this is no time for mealy-mouthed language: *We've got to get back to God or perish.*" Two years later he produces an article on "Not Ashamed of the Gospel,"[28] which had been published in a local paper—the Leicester Evening Mail.

But evangelism was an aspect of the church's contemporary witness regarding which he had misgivings. The first year of his time in Leicester was but half way through when he told his members:

> There seems to be something lacking in our modern school of evangelism. It has got into a rut: its very language has become stereotyped and sloppy. The world must sometimes think of us as a company of "cissies," rather than the Church "terrible and as an army with banners." We are lacking in virility, in courage, in moral fibre.[29]

A characteristic example of how he made application of the bible can be seen when speaking about Ezekiel 24 and the death of Ezekiel's wife, shortly before the close of his ministry:

> I wish that was the only thing that broke your hearts. I wish that you were eaten up with concern for the thousands and thousands of men and women in Leicester who if they were to die tonight are without Christ.
>
> Your energies, your zeal, your love and your fire are for things which will pass away ... your jealousy for church and for nation. Oh, that you would weep. ... for the sins of men and women and only have one passion—

---

[28] *Melbourne Hall Magazine* (November 1949): 201–202.
[29] *Melbourne Hall Magazine* (December 1947): 20.

that they might come to know Christ, whatever the means, whoever has the glory. Even if God comes and sets you aside and says, "Leslie Land, you've had it," "He must increase and I must decrease."[30]

These closing words gain added poignancy knowing that he was aware of the early signs of the illness that foreshadowed what lay ahead.

"Doing an important work"

While Land perhaps would never have abrogated to himself these words of Nehemiah, it is inescapably obvious that he had a deep sense of the significance of the work in which he was engaged, along with a belief that a special blessing had attended it. This was due in part to his general biblical confidence resulting in a recurring emphasis in his ministry that God is working to great ends: "dealing with sin and bringing back the glory that has departed" as he somewhere expressed it. We see this confidence in a sermon on the burning bush, in ways that illustrate his distinctive readiness to develop a line of interpretation and then of unanticipated application. A constant theme throughout his years was that in a context of difficulty, persecution, and secularisation and so on, God is at work *secretly*. Here he says that in the situation of Israelite slavery God "was preparing His man."[31] He interestingly talks of how the bush burned but was not consumed "because the Eternal was in it." There is a "paradox ... stamped on everything in this world that has Christ in it ... It comes in for fire but it is not consumed and out of the very fire there goes forth a message of deliverance and

---

[30] Bible School series on the books of the Old Testament, in 1961.
[31] This and the following quotations are from the *Melbourne Hall Magazine* (March 1949): 137–139.

redemption." Likewise the bible itself "ever burned but it is not consumed." He traces this through the old and new testaments, and to Wycliffe and Tyndale. Similarly for the Church, "humanly speaking the Church is just a common bush—composed of ordinary men and women whom you may meet any day—but God in Christ has chosen to dwell in the midst of her." And "the greater the burning, the clearer and more insistent the message, and men still turn aside to see this great sight" and are saved.

We see a constantly recurring note of specific, spiritually grounded rejoicing in his remarks to the church. We have seen, for example, his gladness of spirit at the growth of spiritual attentiveness and engagement on the part of his young people. The young people reciprocated without hesitation. In the first January of his ministry he offers a thank you to the young people for the gift of "a lovely, huge, shining office typewriter." He adds how encouraged he is: "To see a crowd of young people in the gallery on Sunday is a truly thrilling sight. And to know that you are seeking others and bringing them along to Jesus—well, it's just grand, and God bless you!" The same time saw his custom of sending an open letter to the church members. Although, it was only January 1948, a few months since he commenced his ministry, he could observe "Already God has been pleased to grant us signs of a spiritual revival, which has gladdened all our hearts." Six months later he includes in the magazine extracts from a letter he had received. I reproduce it in some fullness:

Dear Mr. Land,
    You do not know me, although I sit … at Melbourne Hall. I felt I must write this letter to thank you … When I was seventeen I accepted Christ and was baptized and

for three or four years there was none happier than I. Then came the blow, while I was serving in the army; I was injured, my career was ruined and I was discharged. I do not know what happened but it seemed as if in trying to build up a new life I lost touch with God. For two dreary years He was just a shadow. Yet I still went to chapel and tried desperately to hang on to my tottering faith...

Yet never could I seem to penetrate the veil and get near to Him. That is, until last Sunday. It was towards the end of your sermon, and then through your words I suddenly realized what was wrong. I was trying to live like the servant of Elisha. There and then I humbly asked the Master to reconsecrate me, to take possession of my whole life again and do with it as He would.

And then the miracle happened, so marvellous I can never hope to fully describe it. The barriers fell, and like a great light the radiant sunshine of the Saviour seemed to flood every corner of my heart. And the glory of His smile is with me as I write this. We sang that last hymn, "Happy day, happy day," and I am not ashamed to confess that I sang it with a bursting heart and tears in my eyes, for it was a happy day to me, and I went down to that baptismal service as if all the joy in the world had streamed into my soul.

I can never thank you enough for what you have done for me, for I am still in the early twenties and so much lies before. Use this testimony if you wish ... Perhaps it may help someone else.[32]

Well might he say, "I believe we are on the eve of great things for God."

---

[32] *Melbourne Hall Magazine* (July 1948): 77.

Chapter 5
A Preaching Ministry

In encountering Leslie Land as person, pastor, and preacher, we have met him over the first three years. We have seen his ministry marked by a significant blessing through an influx of new members and baptisms; and with Christians, ministers included, travelling from all over the city and county to attend his weekly Bible School.

Preaching was at the heart of what Land consciously saw as the nature and not merely the instrumental means of the gospel. That Land took this view of preaching is not in doubt. Speaking in August 1948 on "The Foolishness of Preaching," included in this book, he starts from the decline of preaching even in some evangelical circles. In words that may be thought to anticipate contemporary images he laments how "The idea commonly held is that preaching is an intrusion upon our worship."[1] On the contrary,

> God has *done* something in history ... But Christmas is not a story in *mime*. God has clothed the drama of our salvation with words. God has spoken. Christianity is no mysticism, no vague aesthetic feeling. It is a revelation made and given in Jesus Christ, made known by a direct preached word ... and all down the ages the power of God has accompanied that preached word, power to

---

[1] This and the following quotations are from the *Melbourne Hall Magazine* (August 1948): 81. Later in his ministry he produced a pamphlet titled, "Expository Preaching and Teaching: Why and How?"

change men's lives,[2] power to "turn the world upside down."

Hence,

The apostles did not go about simply "giving talks." No! One favourite word in the New Testament for *preaching* means to proclaim as a herald, with certainty and authority, demanding—even commanding—a hearing. *Preaching* in the New Testament has all of God behind it.

He refers to the decline of preaching in earlier centuries and how it "became buried beneath a mass of forms and ceremonies, priestly accretions and other external paraphernalia." Then came "the great Protestant reformation"—Luther, Calvin and the reformers—"names to conjure with ... In a word the Reformation was a *rediscovery of the Word of God.*" He rejoiced that he was "free to worship Almighty God in august and dignified simplicity; free from all the tawdry, priestly accretions of those middle ages." It was in this context that he believed, "We need humbly to pray for our many faithful brethren in the State Church."

We are fortunate in being able to gather a full understanding of his preaching, due in part to the extant recordings and also because of the very unusual ways in which he prepared his monthly sermon summaries for the magazine. Indeed, "summary" is the wrong word. They were not synopses. To appreciate this point, we need to know what written notes he took into the pulpit. He had no detailed outline or extended text. Despite the gift from the young people of the "shining office

---

[2] In the universal habit of the time Land uses "man" to refer to humankind in general.

typewriter" it seems that the use of this was reserved for other purposes. His notes were simplicity itself—longhand brief headings in tiny writing on small sheets of paper. The examples given here are from messages on Hebrews 6:1: "Therefore let us leave the elementary doctrine of Christ and go on to maturity," and Genesis 4:3–5: "In the course of time Cain brought to the LORD an offering of the fruit of the ground, and Abel also brought of the firstborn of his flock and of their fat portions. And the LORD had regard for Abel and his offering, but for Cain and his offering he had no regard. So Cain was very angry, and his face fell." They are written on pieces of paper the size of a postcard. It seems to imply that his notes were there as prompts, and that in his messages and studies he drew on an inner store of thoughts and intentions, while the magazine entries seem to be partly transcripts of selected moments in his preaching along with direct recapitulations of the headings from his notes.

His preaching can be expressed as having the following characteristics:

1. Always set in God's wider purposes.
2. A constant eschatological awareness.
3. Marked by pointed application.
4. Often delivered with—and producing in his hearers—a sense of awe.
5. A readiness to develop his own interpretation.
6. An ability to draw from various stylistic and linguistic means to bring spiritual force to bear.
7. An unsentimental but welcoming acceptance of the God-given qualities of humanity.
8. An unflinching faithfulness.

I will work through each of these, taking the liberty of repeating one or two instances from the previous chapters.

1. God's Wider Purposes

Rather like the preaching of Jesus, if the comparison should be made, Land would gently draw hearers into his theme before relating it to God's big picture. It occurs strikingly in his words at the memorial service for the previous minister, Benjamin Gibbon, who died not long after Land arrived in Leicester. He chose to speak on Joshua 1:1–5 ("Moses my servant is dead: now therefore arise, go over this Jordan, thou and all this people … As I was with Moses, so I will be with thee"), in so doing showing he has in mind the succession and not only the past.

Posing the question how God came to choose Benjamin Gibbon, he picks a theme that often recurs in his ministry: "The strange thing is, that all down the ages it has *seemed* as though the worldly setting were the thing that mattered, with religion as a kind of extra for any who happen to have a taste for it."[3] He suggests how the table talk in Egypt would have been about Pharaoh's council decrees, and later about Nineveh, or the glory of Greece. Later "your 'nine o'clock news' would have been Rome—Caesar—the Senate." And "today it is just possible you are tempted to think that what *really* matters is what happened at Geneva—or was it Potsdam?[4] Or is it Moscow, or Washington, or Westminster?"

In contrast, those called "to point men and women to Jesus" were not great men. "They were great because they were

---

[3] This and the following quotation are from the *Melbourne Hall Magazine* (December 1947): 18.

[4] The Soviet leader Joseph Stalin, British Prime Minister Winston Churchill, and U.S. President Harry Truman met in Potsdam, Germany, from July 17 to August 2, 1945, to negotiate terms for the end of World War II.

nothing, and Christ was everything." Like Moses when his face shone it was "because they had communion with God. They had no light of their own."

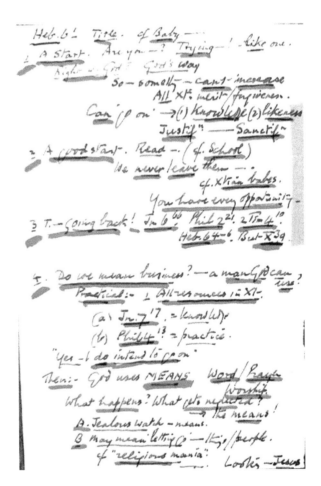

Leslie Land's Sermon Notes 1.0

He took this as his arresting theme at the very end of his Leicester ministry. His final Sunday morning sermon on the opening words of Luke 3—included later in this book—left on the author an indelible impression. To take for a farewell message this decidedly unpromising text on the powers ("hegemonies") of the then world and apply it with such authority and relevance to show how God bypassed the ruling powers, political and ecclesiastical, and spoke through John the Baptist in the wilderness, was for me a revelation. It undergirded the interweaving of light and darkness throughout his ministry. Drawing out elsewhere the application of the Joshua story he says, "The days are grievous, but I believe we are on the eve of great things for God. Yes, amid the confused scene, there is a people waiting to cross over into God's kingdom. 'Arise—go over this Jordan: you and all this people.'"[5]

2. Eschatological Awareness

His sense of the wider picture of God's purposes was linked to an emphasis that was distinctive in his preaching—his sense of living in the end times. This is expressed fully in his *The Appearing of Jesus*—a series of studies given to his weekly Bible School during the last period of his ministry. He drew those studies to a close with the conviction that

> I am going to preach grace while He lends me breath, and I am going to invite sinners whether they are Jews or Gentiles to put their trust in Jesus. You can trust him now. If Jesus comes tonight, at midnight, or in the morning, you will be with him for eternity.[6]

---

[5] *Melbourne Hall Magazine* (December 1947): 20.
[6] W.L. Land, *The Appearing of Jesus* (York: York Publishing Services, 2014): 7.

It permeated his preaching. In a message on "not forsaking the assembling of ourselves," he paused on the phrase "And so much more as you see the day approaching," saying, "Here is a lovely thought—the word translated 'gathering together' is the same word used elsewhere in connection with His Second Advent" (2 Thess. 2:1). ... Here is the choicest, the most urgent reason of all why you and I must not—will not—neglect the gathering of ourselves together. Because we are a 'gathered church' and we await 'a mighty 'gathering together.'"[7] He did not duck the teaching in scripture that "You, brothers, are not in darkness so that this day should surprise you like a thief" (1 Thess. 5:4):

> That day will overtake the world as a thief, but we are not in darkness that it should overtake us quite like that. There is a certain sense in which we can read the signs of the times, but we should do so reverently, discreetly and not in any cranky way. We are children of the light—we are not in the darkness.[8]

But he always warned against looking for times and seasons in the bible: "The bible was never meant to satisfy morbid curiosity, as to times and seasons. It is more like a trusted physician: his job is twofold—diagnosis and cure."[9] He developed this on another occasion:

> I am speaking to those who want to come with a fresh love and simple faith to the Word of God. They do not know all this intricate prophetical detail, this labyrinthine, pigeon-hole detail which has divided even

---

[7] *Melbourne Hall Magazine* (February 1948): 34–35.
[8] Land, *The Appearing of Jesus*, 28.
[9] *Melbourne Hall Magazine* (October 1948): 97.

believers. And I am not sorry that some of them do not know it![10]

3. Pointed Application

We need say little more about Land's pointed *applicatory* style of preaching, but in case the uncomfortable directness of this has been missed, this is how he concludes his message on the foolishness of preaching:

> Shame on us if our preaching has been replaced by a "five-minute talk." Shame on us if our prayers have become flights of pious oratory or vain repetitions. Shame on us if our hymnody has substituted daffodils, subjective phenomena and soppy sentimentalities for the great objective facts of our redeemer and Lord![11]

In the immediacy and heartfelt tone of his preaching, we never gain the impression that he got his application from commentaries or others' sermons.

4. A Sense of Awe

We have observed the sense of *awe* that Land brought to his preaching, and was evoked often in his hearers. It was this that David Kingdon heard during his time as theological editor for the Inter-Varsity Press as lingering in the memories of colleagues in the ministry who had attended his Bible School, and it will bear repeating part of it from the previous chapter:

> One day an elder of the Bethel Evangelical Church, Wigston told me a story which illustrates the impact of that ministry on the lives of many of Leslie Land's hearers. It

---

[10] Land, *The Appearing of Jesus*, 50.
[11] *Melbourne Hall Magazine* (August 1948): 83.

was my friend's custom to attend his weekly Bible School in Melbourne Hall with a group of his friends. More than once such was the sense of awe that came over them that no one spoke in the car as they went home![12]

5. Originality

His originality in approach, interpretation and application also has been evident. His choice of language and figures of speech helped drive through his apt inventiveness. In a relatively lengthy introductory study to the book of Revelation carried in the magazine, his characteristic approach is clear—a deep interest combined with a caution and care. Thus, after comparing the book to the "Deutsches Museum" in Munich and calling the book an apocalyptic gallery, or unveiling, he says:

> 1. This Gallery was not designed by God just to satisfy our curiosity. ... But the main purpose of this apocalyptic Gallery is to inspire all Christians to be faithful and true to the Captain of their salvation.
> 2. The things you see and hear in this Gallery are *symbols* or *signs*... They signify spiritual truth and realities. Do not try to translate everything into dull prose.[13]

He then outlines the book as a series of "halls" in the Gallery. For example, "You will find the first hall of this great Gallery given up to a kind of private interview between the risen Christ and His followers... He is generous with His praise and commendation, but His rebuke is terrible."

---

[12] "Foreword" in Land, *The Appearing of Jesus*, 9
[13] This and the following quotation are from the *Melbourne Hall Magazine* (August 1949): 177–180.

Leslie Land's Sermon Notes 2.0

5. Language and Rhetoric

"Do not try to translate everything into dull prose"[14] was an injunction he did not limit to the message of the book of Revelation. "Dull" is no accident. Not that he thought prose as such was dull, but he persistently brought the power of language to

---

[14] *Melbourne Hall Magazine* (August 1949): 177.

74

bear to persuade his hearers. A common rhetorical device was to build up the force of his argument by repeating a key word. The "Shame on us" quotation above is a good example.[15]

He also would string three or four negatives as a preliminary to drive home the particular point he wanted to make. We see examples of this when he said, dealing with the world post-Hiroshima and Nagasaki: "It is not the *atom* they really fear. It is not science. It is these things in the hand of *man* they fear," and still more powerfully in a message to the Band of Hope that once again bears repeating from Chapter Three:

> I am not concerned merely with the "alcoholic"—the poor man or woman in the grip of that awful disease—I am not concerned only with men and women who, otherwise gifted and talented, are sapping and destroying their mental powers and prospects with this accursed habit—I am not thinking only of broken, ruined homes and marriages, or of the crime of cultivating acres for brewing purposes when nations, women and children are perishing for want of wheat and bread. No, I am thinking rather of a level of life which is the best that multitudes of our fellow men and women know—a life roofed in by *this* world—a life which misses the goal and purpose for which Almighty God created men—a life which ends, like the book of Genesis, "in a coffin in Egypt."[16]

---

[15] This rhetorical device is known as *anaphora,* and he employed it on several occasions. This and the following quotation are both from *Melbourne Hall Magazine* (October 1947): 4–6).

[16] *Melbourne Hall Magazine* (November 1947): 11.

6. An Unsentimental but Welcoming Acceptance
of the God-Given Qualities of Humanity

The interweaving of darkness and light to which we have referred mirrored his view of humanity. When he speaks of the world of science he retains deep respect for the creativity of humanity alongside the recognition of the potential for harm it brings. A sermon he calls "The New Look," reprinted later in this book, illustrates both his readiness to welcome the qualities of humanity and his distinctive mastery of the English language. In using the phrase "The New Look" he has picked up a fashion chain name, still present today, and turns to the verse "They looked unto Him and were lightened" (Ps. 34:5). He then took the idea of becoming like what we love, and the transforming consequences of looking to and meeting Christ: "As a sinner and his new-found Saviour walk and talk together day by day, there steals a likeness, a Christ-likeness, into the heart and into the look." He found everyday metaphors to make his point:

> Have you ever looked down in your garden at some shapeless, lifeless, motionless thing, and then, all at once, *it moves* … "It's alive!" Well, it's possible for years to go on toying with a dead religion, a creed, a code of ethics, and then—all at once one day to meet Christ. "It's alive!" "He's alive!" Anything may happen.[17]

He further developed his point by saying "Christ brings not only a new look, but a new way of *looking,* a new way of looking at other men and women" as "men and women for whom Christ died." Yet "I do not believe that conversion renders any

---

[17] This and the following quotation are from the *Melbourne Hall Magazine* (May 1948): 58.

man unnatural or unsexed; nay, rather … human love, human relationships, human laughter are all enriched and enhanced when Christ is in them." Not that he held sentimental attachments to the experience of daily life. Speaking in the 1949 New Year on Matthew 2:12, also included in this book, he says we have seen the Christ, "we have had an encounter with the God-Saviour." Now "we must return to 'our own country,' we must return to the humdrum and toil of everyday life, but we must surely return 'another way' … We cannot, we simply cannot go back to the old life."[18]

Finally, this new look "knows how to look out on the future." While Christians are never uninterested in what, for example, Russia and America will do—indeed, he insists, a Christian should be more intelligently interested in world affairs than someone who is not a Christian—we "travel light."

7. Unflinching Faithfulness

Aspects of these various characteristics can be found throughout his preaching. Two final examples will suffice, and in so doing also illustrate his unwavering faithfulness. First, a message on "the earnest of our inheritance" (Eph. 1:4), is a good illustration of how he structured his preaching and unfolded and applied a theme. Second, his message on "the sign of Jonah" (Luke 11:29–36), shows once again how he saw the times and the challenge for Christians.

"The earnest of our inheritance"
His message from Ephesians starts with an explanation of "earnest":

---

[18] *Melbourne Hall Magazine* (January 1949): 121.

it probably had its origin from the Phoenician traders. A transaction would be made and one party would hand over to the other "earnest money," a part payment. It established the deal ... It was more than an installment, it was a pledge and guarantee that the remainder would, in due course, be honoured and paid over.[19]

After a comment on the verse he says:

Will you notice three simple, yet wonderful things about this earnest of our salvation? (1) It is an installment of the *same kind* as the full and final inheritance. The believer in Christ possesses life of the *same kind* as the life to be. The spiritual life of the true Christian is the same in kind as the glorified life hereafter, the same in *kind* though not in degree or glory.'

He observes,

Oh I know we Christians too seldom and too little display this real installment. The disparity, the discrepancy is *not* a challenge to the truth of God's Word, it's a challenge to *us* who profess and call ourselves *Christians*. ...

(2) But while the earnest installment is the same in kind, we note, secondly, this is only *an installment*. The same in kind but only a tiny fraction in degree of the full and final inheritance. It has not, as yet, entered into man's heart what good things God has prepared for them that love Him ...

(3) This "*earnest*" implies not only present privilege and guarantee, it also implies *obligation*. We are in danger of forgetting this. In accepting the earnest-money, you knowingly and solemnly place yourself under an

---

[19] The quotations from this message are from the *Melbourne Hall Magazine* (March 1950): 233. The article is reprinted in this book.

obligation to go through with the transaction. ... [Hence] You are not your own, you are bought with a price ... You cannot, you simply *cannot* go back to the world. To do so is to insult the Spirit of grace and to trample under foot the Son of God.

He concludes by saying, "The Gospel brings unspeakable privileges and 'untellable' prospects of glory, but may God, the Holy Spirit, remind us that it brings solemn responsibilities and obligations also."

"The sign of Jonah"
Knowing what we do regarding his approach to the last things, his downplaying of reading signs of such things in the contemporary world is all we may expect. "It is interesting to recall that these early sign-seekers were surrounded by signs... Strange blindness of the human heart: Christ-rejecters ever seek a sign!" Quoting Jesus' words that there will be no other sign but Jonah, he remarks, "There is evidently a 'mystery' as well as a history in the story of the prophet Jonah. No other sign but the sign of the prophet Jonah! In other words, the Cross and the resurrection of Jesus Christ are God's last words to mankind before the Judgment."[20]

He returns to one of his main themes—the state of the times: "We are witnessing in our time a darkness—a spiritual and moral darkness—in many ways unsurpassed in history, and this in spite of our tremendous advance in knowledge and human wisdom." It is "affecting every sphere and every phase of our modern life. It is manifest in our modern attitude to labour and toil, in our art and films and modern music."

---

[20] The following extracts from this sermon are from the *Melbourne Hall Magazine* (May 1949): 153–155.

Yet he is never a mere doomsayer. He values advances in knowledge and always has his science education in the back of his mind. Also he makes the interesting remark that:

> It is true that in certain thinking quarters there are signs of an awakening, signs of a hopeful kind of despair—the despair that leads to salvation. Thinking men, unlikely men, are coming to realize that man's spiritual eye has long been focused on the wrong object.

He applies his message to Christians as well as those who are not:

> What are we to say to these things? What are we going to do about it? Well, as the church of Jesus Christ we better take to heart His words, "There shall no sign be given them but the sign of the prophet Jonah" ... Our Christian business is to proclaim the sign and demonstrate its power in our daily lives.

It would be redundant to speak of his faithfulness were it not so central to the man and his identity. We will see this further evidenced in the following chapter, where we focus on the closing years of his ministry.

Chapter 6
A Complete Ministry

Having spent extended time with Leslie Land during the opening years of his period in Leicester, we have seen how the hall-
marks of his ministry were established early. While they did
not change, his concern to speak to the circumstances and
needs of the day meant that the way he applied the gospel was
shaped by his sense of the pastoral and spiritual needs of the
church, and wider developments in church and nation.

The turn of the decade—the late 1950s through to the 60s—
were years when the consequences of the Second World War
lingered, but new directions were taken nationally and inter-
nationally. 1960 was the year when the USA first sent troops
into Vietnam, and when the USA's U2 spy plane was shot
down by the Soviet Union, bringing the two powers to the edge
of conflict. Refugee problems still continued across Europe, as
well as in China and Hong Kong, and Melbourne Hall more
than once sent substantial gifts. 1959–1960 was World Refugee
year. The ill-fated American-backed invasion of Cuba in the
"Bay of Pigs" episode took place in April 1961, and the Berlin
Wall was erected from August. In the ecclesiastical world the
ecumenical movement was gaining momentum. There was an
anonymous Q and A piece in March 1961, probably by Leslie
Land, on "What can the Archbishop of Canterbury hope to
achieve by his visit to the Pope?" Geoffrey Fisher made the visit

in December 1960.[1] He feared it would prove a visit for which "our nation stands to gain nothing but to lose much."[2]

Land sustained a concern regarding such wider movements in the world. An organisation called The Gospel Publicity League, based in New South Wales, had issued an appeal to America and "the Christian World" to convey a most solemn warning. Land included the "Appeal" in an issue of the magazine. As I write, the outworkings of the 2022 Russian invasion of Ukraine are not clear. The words of this 1961 "Appeal," while directed to the West, have continuing relevance: "Upon you, as Ministers set in authority, and Leaders of Church and State, and you as citizens, there is a heavy responsibility as we near the precipice of a *third* world conflict."[3]

He would have concurred with words spoken by Sidney Lawrence, the minister of a daughter church that we will have reason to mention later. Preaching at Melbourne Hall, Sidney Lawrence, speaking on Jesus' words "he that endures to the end shall be saved," says that in these words Jesus is telling us that

> as Christians we not only share the trials that are common to (all people). We are to expect further suffering just because we *are* Christians. Let us never fall into the error of offering Christ as One who will give us a happy, comfortable and easy life and save us from things we do not like![4]

---

[1] Geoffrey Fisher was Archbishop of Canterbury from 1945 to 1961. He became the first Archbishop of Canterbury to meet a Pope since the Reformation.

[2] *Melbourne Hall Magazine* (March 1961): 211.

[3] *Melbourne Hall Magazine* (August 1961): 271.

[4] This and the following quotation are by Sidney Lawrence, preaching on "He that endures to the end shall be saved," in *Melbourne Hall Magazine* (January 1960): 40, 42.

We are to endure, to hold out, to be among those here and there who are standing alone, "to remain or stay behind when others have departed," as he paraphrases the term. In an application that may apply in any year, he concludes "May God enable us in 1960 and in every subsequent year to endure, to stay on, remain behind when others have given up, continuing on through every trial."

During these years Land's ministry continued to be blessed. Over the period from October 1959 to the end of his time at Melbourne Hall in December 1961, he baptised 55 people and 52 were admitted to membership. As 1960 began he recorded that during the year "many have been baptised into Christ."[5] He observed during the 1950s that wherever he went

> again and again I find that your faith, your love for Jesus Christ has sounded abroad and that all kinds of men and women, boys and girls, are feeling the impact of the work of grace that is going on in the hearts and lives of so many here at Melbourne Hall, Leicester.[6]

In May 1961 Leslie Land was beginning the fifteenth year of his ministry. The church had always employed a deaconess Sister. Sister Florence writes in this issue,

> We thank you for all that under God, you have meant to so many. May all the riches of God's grace and presence and power be with you constantly throughout another year. Thus may you share in the joy that was Paul's, in knowing that the gospel has come to us to whom you

---

[5] *Melbourne Hall Magazine* (January 1960): 39.
[6] *Melbourne Hall Magazine* (June 1956): 385.

minister "not in word only, but also in power, and in the Holy Ghost, and in much assurance."[7]

Presumably no-one, perhaps including Land, was to know that this would be the final annual anniversary of his arrival.

Themes and Grace Notes

Throughout this period, he continued to explain and apply God's word to urgently warn against formal, nominal, half-hearted professions of faith. Speaking in October 1959 on Paul's words, "That I may gain Christ" (Phil. 3:7–8), he pointed out that the word "gain" in verse 7 is the same basic word as "win" in verse 8 of the King James version.[8] He went on to observe, in characteristic words, that

> quite honestly it is *not* true of the average person's experience of religion. Who could say that it is worthwhile to part with anything and everything in order to share the experience of a merely nominal go-to-church-on-Sunday kind of Christian profession? But Paul is talking of something real, living, vital. He is speaking of Christ.[9]

He spoke of the "gain" as a great deliverance, a free access to God, a renewed nature, a never-failing treasury and an eternal inheritance, and urged his hearers, "Do not rest until you have gained Christ." He would often read parts of hymns within his preaching. In February 1960, he ended with a verse from a hymn by Charles Wesley:

---

[7] Sister Florence was the Deaconess Sister at Melbourne Hall for most of Leslie Land's ministry. *Melbourne Hall Magazine* (May 196)1: 234.

[8] The word is translated "gain" in both verses of the ESV

[9] This and the following quotation are from the *Melbourne Hall Magazine* (October 1959).

O Thou who camest from above
The pure celestial fire to impart,
Kindle a flame of sacred love
On the mean altar of my heart.

The various themes of his preaching were interwoven, the one finding force from the other. For example, in May 1961 when speaking on "God's Forgiveness," he asks, "Why are there so few *converted* Christians?" His reply:

> The answer is that in the professing church there prevails (and has prevailed for a long time) a vague general notion about God's forgiveness which is far removed from the revelation concerning forgiveness given in God's Word. It is a vague, woolly notion that God is a kind, amiable being who will in any case forgive everybody anything. It has come about largely through a famine of faithful Bible preaching and teaching.[10]

In the final weeks of his ministry he showed how being taken up with Christ brings pastoral comfort. Speaking from "He shall not see death" (John 8:51), he dealt with the Christian and physical death. Recognising that "timorous mortals start and shrink to cross the narrow sea,"[11] he argues that when Jesus says "Truly, truly, I say to you, if anyone keeps my word, he will never see death," he says "in effect, that those whose hearts and minds are taken up with him and his word, will not *notice* physical death when it comes ... They will not notice, not focus

---

[10] *Melbourne Hall Magazine* (May 1961): 232.
[11] This is a couplet from Isaac Watts' hymn, "A Prospect of Heaven Makes Death Easy."

their eyes upon, death when it comes."[12] This, "is just a particular application of a more general biblical principle, 'You keep him in perfect peace whose mind is stayed on you, because he trusts in you.'"

As his ministry entered the final two years, his characteristic seriousness became, if anything, more marked. On one occasion he gave out the title "The Fool says 'Tomorrow': the Holy Spirit says 'Today'" (from Luke 12 and Hebrews 3:7). He tells his readers and hearers that the reasons the Holy Spirit says "Today" are because of the fact of death, judgement, and the promise of life eternal.

We have seen in Chapter Two an exchange of letters with Martyn Lloyd-Jones, two decades before he was speaking on this later occasion, when they were sharing thoughts on the work of the American theologian, Reinhold Niebuhr. Land quotes here Niebuhr's words:

"We thought," said the two travellers on the road to Emmaus. "We thought," says the modern mind, "that a God without wrath brought men without sin into a kingdom without judgement through a Christ without a Cross."[13]

It is possible that this was linked with an awareness on his part that not everyone was wholly with him. Speaking in 1960 on the tongue as "set on fire by hell" (Ja. 3:16), he says that the tongue is a fire in three senses:

Because of its *heat*. The tongue is the instrument of wrath, strife and contention ... Because of its *danger* ...

---

[12] This and the following quotation are from the *Melbourne Hall Magazine* (November 1961): 304.

[13] *Melbourne Hall Magazine* (September 1960): 136.

The tongue is a fire. It destroys lives and characters; it turns houses, churches, nations into a wilderness. Because it *wounds*. These wounds are very painful. Sometimes they fester and never heal.[14]

He goes on to lament that "you will find this unhallowed fire burning in almost every sanctuary of God. It is to this day the biggest curse in church life," and "this great evil is very difficult to cure. It is very certain that mere association with some religious movement—however evangelical—will not do it. Nor will a mental or intellectual assent to evangelical belief avail anything."

It was on this occasion that he spoke words we have noted previously: "Oh, how I know that it is not easy or pleasant to have to say these things, and it does not make for popularity. But ... faithfulness, not popularity will count in the day of Christ." One can detect an implied application to his own time when he imagines, speaking on another occasion on Noah, a "preacher of righteousness," that people would not listen to him. "'Silly old-fashioned evangelical,' they would say. "Why doesn't he move on with the times in his preaching? Fancy preaching *sin* and *judgement*."[15] He spoke in a similar way in one of his messages on the final appearing of Jesus:

Satan has coined ... the word "Fundamentalist." If anyone calls you a Fundamentalist you are supposed to shrink, shrivel and apologise! If you are a Fundamentalist you will be laughed at. I agree that Satan has captured a little truth in it. He always makes sure of that. There are some wooden-headed Christians who have been cranky

---

[14] This and the following quotation are from the *Melbourne Hall Magazine* (February 1960): 51–53.

[15] *Melbourne Hall Magazine* (August 1961): 268–269.

about their exposition of some of these precious doctrines, and have given cause for ridicule. So Satan frightens others by that. At its best, however, to be a Fundamentalist means you believe what God's word says. You believe the great, fundamental doctrines of the Christian faith without any apology or vaporising them away.[16]

In all of this Leslie Land was what we may call a "big picture" man, whether about the church or the world as a whole. For example, when speaking on "Are You Called?"—a message that appears in this book—we can detect that although he may be speaking primarily to the individual, he does so in ways that resonate with the whole-hearted commitment to missionary work that we return to below, and with an underlying message about how a local church should be understood in the light of the New Testament. Again, in a message he called "Axes and Saws" from words in Isaiah 10:15: "Shall the axe boast over him who hews with it, or the saw magnify itself against him who wields it?" he deals with how the great powers of the world are "axes and saws. They are for chastisement; they are for disciplining and the shaping of the living stones".[17] He gave this message in the summer months of 1961 in the context of the international tensions over the "Bay of Pigs" episode, mentioned earlier.

There is a recurring emphasis of his ministry conveying a sense that God is working to great ends—"dealing with sin and bringing back the glory that has departed" as we have quoted him saying. We saw a characteristic example in Chapter Four of how he made application of the bible, when speaking about

---

[16] Land, *The Appearing of Jesus*, Chapter 6.
[17] *Melbourne Hall Magazine* (October, 1961): 294. This was one of the messages that he subsequently produced as a pamphlet.

Ezekiel 24 and the death of Ezekiel's wife, but perhaps the most memorable instance was the message he called 'Hegemony', on the unpromising opening words of Luke 3. The first two verses read:

> In the fifteenth year of the reign of Tiberius Caesar, Pontius Pilate being governor of Judea, and Herod being tetrarch of Galilee, and his brother Philip tetrarch of the region of Ituraea and Trachonitis, and Lysanias tetrarch of Abilene during the high priesthood of Annas and Caiaphas, the word of God came to John the son of Zechariah in the wilderness.

This was his final Sunday morning message and the only sermon text that appeared twice in the church magazine during his fourteen years at the church. It appears later in this book, but part of his introduction bears repeating here:

> The Greek word translated "reign" has come over into our English dictionaries. It is the word 'hegemony.' It means powerful leadership, mastery, domination. Now let us read Luke's dull verses again: "In the fifteenth year of the hegemony or world domination of Tiberius Caesar, Pontius Pilate being delegated to the hegemony of Judea, and Herod, Philip and Lysanias being vassals of this hegemony, Annas and Caiaphas being the hierarchy of the hegemony over Judaism and the Jewish people." If you are not awestruck and impressed, you must indeed have been to Calvary's cross and had all your values changed.[18]

---

[18] *Melbourne Hall Magazine* (January 1962): 327.

A related characteristic of his preaching was how he would sometimes take an unlikely, perhaps difficult text and speak with what we may call expository ingenuity. For example, a sermon on the difficult verse in 1 Peter 3:20 about being "saved by water," becomes a means of taking his hearers into the heart of the gospel of having a "good conscience toward God." He did much the same when speaking from the book of Esther in what would prove to be his final Easter message. He manages to make the story of the book of Esther the basis for his message, playing on the Septuagint translation of the judgement on Haman on the gallows he had erected for Mordecai, as "Let him be crucified." As the tables were turned on Haman, so, he reminds us, at Easter God turned the tables on Satan in the crucifixion of Jesus.

Notwithstanding the seriousness of tone, Land manifestly delighted in preaching the grace of God. Speaking at Christmas in 1960 he gave a brief message from Luke 2:11. He concludes that, "As the years go by, I am increasingly conscious of two things: 1. I deserve none of these things. 2. The grace of God has appeared bringing salvation." He observes "Little wonder that preaching becomes more wonderful—or is it the Christ we preach?"[19]

His confidence in God's gospel appears again when six months later he chose the closing words of the Old Testament, "before that dreadful day comes." He takes the prophecy of Malachi that God would send "Elijah the prophet," explaining that, "We have here one of those divine prophecies which have several successive fulfilments."[20] He then applies it saying,

---

[19] *Melbourne Hall Magazine* (December 1960): 171.
[20] The quotations on this page are from the *Melbourne Hall Magazine* (June 1961): 243–244.

In the great Reformation of the sixteenth century, the reformers Luther, Calvin, Knox and others, came in the spirit and power of Elijah. In the eighteenth century we find another fulfilment of this precious prophetic provision in Wesley, Whitefield and Edwards.

Hence, "this is the gracious gospel which God makes known through his messengers—coming in the spirit and power of Elijah—before his judgment falls. It warns, it woos, it offers Christ."

He concludes saying,

> we pray and long for it to happen in our land, and indeed throughout the world, on a scale and in a manner which we have come to associate historically with revivals, before the coming of the great and dreadful day of the Lord.

Time and again he unsettles our expectations, taking in this case a verse of judgement and making it a prayer for revival. One of his sermons on revival is included in this book.

Looking Outwards

We have seen much of the direction of Land's wide spiritual gaze in the previous chapters. His own reading, the recommendations and examples he placed before others, and the network of people in which he found his home, all give pointers.

Reading

The frequent recommendations of good books, including the latest publications of the *Banner of Truth Trust*, tucked away in the pages of his monthly magazine and on the church bookstall, and the string of good preachers occupying his pulpit whenever he was away, were alike testimony to his quiet determination. Readers would also come across Charles Spurgeon's "Precepts for Ministerial Students," J. I. Packer on "The Plan of God," an extract from J.C. Ryle on "Defective Evangelism," Alan Stibbs on "Parenthood" and Brownlow North's 'Six Rules for Young Christians' in the pages of the church's monthly magazine. I have little doubt that it was his own action that lay behind a note in the magazine in March 1960 to the effect that "In answer to a special request the Leicestershire County library have (*sic*) kindly purchased the following good and rare books"—Jonathan Edwards' *Life and Diary of David Brainerd*, John Owen's *The Glory of Christ*, Isaac Watts' *The World to Come*, and *The Letters of Samuel Rutherford*. These, along with Andrew Bonar's *Memoirs of M'Cheyne*, were repeated in another magazine in a list of "Good Books," along with information about where they could be purchased.

On a further occasion he included a note recommending, as Christmas gifts: A subscription to the Evangelical Magazine ("Edited by Dr James Packer");[21] *The Sermon on the Mount* Martyn Lloyd-Jones; *Expository Thoughts on the Gospels*, J.C. Ryle; *Doing and Daring* on the History of Melbourne Hall.

The main piece in the May 1960 magazine was the extract from J.C. Ryle on "Defective Evangelism." The covering note illuminates Land's concerns. He takes the opportunity to tell readers that the book can be obtained from the Banner of Truth offices ("price 13/6, 14/8 by post"). "Ryle's remarks," he observes, "appear to have been prompted by the revival movement which began about 1873 and which was accompanied by

---

[21] The Evangelical Magazine was edited by Elizabeth Braund and was a major source of biblical writing in the 1950s and 1960s. For example, the book, *Knowing God,* by J.I. Packer, had its origin in an extended series of articles in this magazine. An obituary can be found at www.evangelical-times.org/elizabeth-braund-1921-2013. She wrote about her life in Elizabeth Braund, *The Young Woman Who Lived in a Shoe* (London: Pickering and Inglis, 1984).

a new emphasis in evangelism."[22] He had addressed questions of evangelism through two extracts from Martyn Lloyd-Jones in the summer of 1956. It may have been that he felt it easier to raise such questions indirectly, through the words of others such as Lloyd-Jones and Ryle. Having said this, he was happy for the church to organise a coach trip to hear Billy Graham preach in Manchester in June 1961.

His reading can also be mapped through the constant extracts—brief and long—that appeared in the magazine over this period. There were long leading articles, as we have seen in part, by Alan Redpath, Alan Stibbs, J.C. Ryle, J.I. Packer and Martyn Lloyd-Jones, and briefer pointed paragraphs from writers such as Andrew Murray, Brownlow North, C.H. Spurgeon, Handley Moule, Robert Murray M'Cheyne, Theo Bamber[23] and Bishop Ellicott.[24]

People

We have seen that one of the reasons he gave for ending his ministry in 1961 was to allow him to respond more freely to invitations. Early in 1960 he scanned his diary and spoke of how his wider ministry continued in the year ahead. He was scheduled to speak at Westminster Chapel—an annual occasion for most of his ministry—Cambridge University and another university Christian Union, the Southern Counties Convention, a grammar school, five other churches, and the annual conference of the Pocket Testament League.[25] At different times during 1961 he records that he was to preach "in my old

---

[22] *Melbourne Hall Magazine* (May 1960): 87.

[23] A Baptist minister in Rye Lane Chapel, London, from 1926 to 1961.

[24] A vicar in the Church of England, Professor of Divinity in London and then Cambridge, and Bishop of Gloucester.

[25] Pocket Gospels for Evangelism | The Pocket Testament League (ptluk.org).

university (Oxford)"[26] and at Keele University College (as Keele University then was called) and again in Westminster Chapel, along with two well-known evangelical churches, and Nottingham and Manchester Universities.

He spoke early in 1960 at the Theological Students' Conference on "Evangelistic Preaching." His seriousness of tone in preaching in no way reflected a pessimism regarding the gospel. His reflection on this conference was, "It was indeed heartwarming to see clear signs of a very definite return to sound biblical theology and teaching. Such a response would scarcely have been possible a few years ago. Thank God for this light on the horizon."[27]

Among the visitors to the Melbourne Hall pulpit or midweek meetings, Marj Saint, the widow of Nate Saint, one of the five American missionaries to Ecuador, martyred in 1956, spoke at the end of 1959. Another notable visitor to a Bible School was Omri Jenkins, then Home Director of the European Missionary Fellowship.[28] Martyn Lloyd-Jones was visiting for a mid-week service for the daughter church in March. In June 1961 Ernest Kevan, then Principal of the London Bible College, was to pay one of his occasional preaching visits.

Hidden away in October 1961 is a note that John Blanchard (1932–2021) was to speak in the church at a meeting known as "Christian Endeavour." He was then only 28.[29]

---

[26] *Melbourne Hall Magazine* (May 1961): 234.

[27] *Melbourne Hall Magazine* (February 1960): 56.

[28] Now the European Mission Fellowship (www.europeanmission.org). The tributes to Omri Jenkins (1915–2003) at www.evangelical-times.org/omri-jenkins-1915-2003 and www.banneroftruth.org/uk/resources/articles/2003/t-omri-jenkins-1915-2003 well repay reading. He can be heard preaching at, for example, www.emw.org.uk/1985/08/t-omri-jenkins-aber-1985-1.

[29] www.banneroftruth.org/uk/about/banner-authors/john-blanchard.

Among the reprinted articles were some by those who were peers of Land. One could say more about each of these, but I will limit myself to one significant figure who is much less known and remembered than should be the case: Alan Stibbs (1901–1971). After time on the mission field in China, his preaching and teaching led him to the staff of Oakhill Theological College in London, and he became known as a Bible expositor and preacher in demand for evangelical conferences and conventions. John Stott said of him, "Alan Stibbs was a voice crying in the wilderness, a lonely evangelical scholar in a sea of liberalism. We owe him much."[30] We do indeed.

In October 1959 there was a "Recognition" service at Melbourne Hall for the induction of Sidney Lawrence as minister of the daughter church, at which Paul Tucker, Minister of East London Tabernacle,[31] was to give what Land later described as "a mighty message from God's word."[32]

There were key figures closely associated within the Melbourne Hall fellowship. Margaret Manton, for example, had been awarded the Churchill Prize for Biblical Knowledge at the London Bible College (now the London School of Theology) in 1959.[33] We notice others below.

---

[30] A valuable collection of his shorter writings can be found in a book edited by Andrew Atherstone, *So Great Salvation: The Collected Essays of Alan Stibbs* (Fearn: Christian Focus Publications, 2008).

[31] Paul Tucker was the minister of East London Tabernacle from 1954. A helpful history of the church can be seen at www.eltbaptistchurch.org/about/our-history tracing the links back to its association with Charles Spurgeon. He left East London Tabernacle to become minister of Portadown Baptist Church in North Ireland form 1973 until his retirement on health grounds in 1983.

[32] *Melbourne Hall Magazine* (November 1959): 17.

[33] It was courtesy of Margaret Manton that I was able to write the material on Land's friendship with Martyn Lloyd-Jones. She had been able to preserve Lloyd-Jones' letter to Land written mainly during the Second World War, later given to the Banner of Truth Trust.

His concern for encouraging good preaching was noticeable in the final weeks of his ministry. He placed a note in the magazine in 1961 asking, "will all lay preachers of our church and congregation kindly meet me at the manse on Friday 20 October, at 8pm."[34] The following two months saw the outworking of this meeting. The November magazine records that a "Lay Preachers' Fellowship" was formed at the meeting previously announced. Wasting no time, "Mr Land, as Chairman, addressed the meeting on 'Preaching Today.' An informal discussion followed."[35] A further meeting took place on December 8, when notice was given that the speaker would be "Rev Dr James Packer of Oxford."

It is not clear whether the Fellowship continued. Shortly after he left there was a note in the March 1962 magazine that a meeting had been called "to determine the future organisation of the fellowship, and to discuss certain problems which may arise in connection with it. However, it is hoped that, during the course of the evening, the Rev T. Hughie Jones will be speaking on the problems arising from local loyalties and outside engagements."[36] No report on the visit of Packer was given.

Fields of Mission Church Planting

There were endeavours to plant new churches. The most prominent one being the work that became Knighton Free Church. The church became established with the call of Sidney

---

[34] *Melbourne Hall Magazine* (October 1961): 296.
[35] How one would wish to have heard him! The emphases he would have placed are no doubt reflected in the two pieces, one of which is included in this book: 'The Folly of What We Preach" and "Expository Preaching and Teaching: Why and How?"
[36] *Melbourne Hall Magazine* (March 1962): 355.

Lawrence as the minister.[37] He had been in the ministry for some twelve years at the time of his call, and had seceded from a mainline denomination.

Sidney Lawrence's early ministry at Knighton was seeing encouraging blessings. He soon identified steadily increasing congregations, growing attendances at midweek bible study and prayer meetings, a Sunday School "expanding almost weekly,"[38] and increased weekly offerings, of which a tithe was being given to missionary work.

The relationship between Melbourne Hall and Knighton continued close, certainly enriched by the personal relationship between the ministers. Lawrence preached at Melbourne Hall several times including when Land was at what seems to have been an almost annual engagement, preaching at the Southern Counties Convention over a week. He also took an occasional Bible School. Herbert Carson, who also seceded, this time from the Church of England, followed Sidney Lawrence as minister of the church in 1982.[39]

The Mission Field

At the opening of this chapter, we saw the wholehearted commitment to missionary work manifested by Land. He led this

---

[37] The opening part of the 'Recognition' service can be heard at Induction of Rev SJ Lawrence 1 (https://knighton.org.uk/sermons/induction-of-rev-sj-lawrence-1). The photograph of Sidney Lawrence is taken from that site. This is one of the very few public access sites where Land can be heard.

[38] *Melbourne Hall Magazine* (April 1960): 79.

[39] Herbert Carson (1922–2003) was Vicar of St Paul's, Cambridge, for seven years from 1958. He resigned the living of St Paul's in December 1964, and seceded from Anglicanism, because of misgivings about liturgy, Establishment, bishops, and infant baptism. He assisted Martyn Lloyd-Jones at Westminster Chapel London, before becoming minister of Hamilton Road Baptist Church, Bangor, in 1967. He was chairman of Evangelical Press, Darlington, during the 1970s. In 1982, he moved to become minister of Knighton Evangelical Free Church, Leicester, and retired in 1988. His Farewell to Anglicanism, 1969, gave an account of this period of his life.

with utter conviction and determination. It was not until the following decade that reformed churches in the UK—and they probably would not have routinely used that descriptive term—began to recognise ways in which the New Testament included regulative principles and practices for the local church. But Land's commitment to thinking through the biblical basis of missionary work was unbending. The contributions in this book on "Are You Called?" and, more explicitly, "The Missionary Call and the Local Church," are central to this.

Month after month the sixteen-page, closely typeset magazine would devote anything from one to four pages of reports from the missionaries supported by the church. From 1956 he set the church the vision of financially supporting 100 per cent those who had gone out. He was supported in important ways by the presence of people like John Dean, who worked initially with the Scripture Union in northern Nigeria and had a formative influence on a number of young men who would play a part in the indigenous church.[40] George Burton was another widely respected figure who preached on occasion at Melbourne Hall when home from the mission field and wrote in the magazine. The writing for the magazine by these and others would often extend well beyond missionary *reportage.*

John ("Jack") Sperry (1924–2012), who became the third Bishop of the Arctic, is an example of how Land was able to keep links across boundaries. He spoke and wrote constantly for the information and blessing of the church. One website

---

[40] John Dean is among the significant number of people whose names and memories have suffered through the way that the advent of the Internet and search engines such as Google have paradoxically buried the part played by those who lived and worked in the immediately preceding generations. An integration of his contributions to the Melbourne Hall magazine would help rescue him from Western obscurity.

records that "Sperry was a critic of the social liberalism that seeped up from southern Canada. While accepting women priests, he and his conservative parishioners remained strongly critical of abortion and extramarital sex and created controversy in 2005 when the diocese banned the employment of 'homosexuals, lesbians and bisexuals.'" A week before his death, he was awarded the Queen's Diamond Jubilee Medal. The Press apparently called him "the Billy Graham of the Arctic."[41] The direction of travel was not one way, from missionary to church. For example, the Easter morning services were recorded, and copies sent out to all the fourteen missionaries supported by the church, along with audio-recorded greetings from friends and relatives in the church.

The giving was largely in accord with this vision. The annual missionary giving for 1960 was at the equivalent of over $66000 (£50000) at current values, and a marked increase from the 1956 giving which was at the equivalent of $46000.

Land also established an annual "Missionary Convention" when speakers such as Omri Jenkins and Leslie Lyall[42] were invited alongside those from the church who were in the UK. Several of these names occur in the final missionary convention, which was richly served with speakers. John Savage, the

---

[41] See, among several sources, John Sperry, Pioneer Bishop (https://livingchurch.org/2012/03/12/john-sperry-pioneer-bishop), Our Ordinariate Remembers Bishop John Sperry—The Anglican Church of Canada (www.anglican.ca/news/our-ordinariate-remembers-bishop-john-sperry/30032325), Former Anglican bishop of Arctic, John Reginald Sperry, dies at 87 (www.anglicannews.org/news/2012/02/former-anglican-bishop-of-arctic,-john-reginald-sperry,-dies-at-87.aspx) and "He fought the good fight with humour and skill" (https://www.smh.com.au/national/he-fought-the-good-fight-with-humour-and-skill-20120228-1u0rf.html). In 2001, Sperry published a memoir, *Igloo Dwellers Were My Church*. (Calgary, AL: Bayeux Arts Inc., 2001).

[42] Leslie Lyall was a missionary in China, prolific author, and latterly on the staff of the then China Inland Mission. See https://bdcconline.net/en/stories/lyall-leslie-theodore.

General Secretary of the Evangelical Union of South America,[43] whose name appears as part of the responses to Land's writing on the support of missionaries elsewhere in this book, Omri Jenkins from the European Missionary Fellowship, John Dean and 'Archdeacon John Sperry', all were present.

"Thank you, Mr Land, for preaching Christ"

Without any previous hint, the December 1961 church magazine contains a letter. I reproduce it here in full.

The Manse

Nov. 25th 1961

Dear Christian friends,

As I told my elders mid-November and announced from the pulpit last Sunday, I believe the time has come when I can and should lay down my office as minister of Melbourne Hall.

When I came to you in 1947, I said that I thought no-one should hold such an office for more than ten years. I have been here fourteen and a half years. They have been very happy years and God has very graciously blessed the preaching and teaching of his holy word.

I receive an ever-increasing number of requests to preach in other centres (churches, universities, conferences, etc) up and down our land. It is now very clear to me that I should be free to take a fuller part in this wider ministry. The future is in God's good hands; we take a step at a time, in faith. My ministry at Melbourne Hall will end on the 31st December.

---

[43] The Evangelical Union of South America, founded in 1911, became Latin Link in 1991 on merging with the Regions Beyond Missionary Union. There is information on the origins of the mission at https://archiveshub.jisc.ac.uk/search/archives/fc8c2a0c-bee8-3b1a-87a0-08fdc8fffcc2#:~:text=EUSA%20was%20formed%20from%20three,two%20years%20later%20in%201913).

Thank you for the many kind and gracious letters already received. It is a joy to know that many of you were "born again" during my ministry, while many have been drawn closer to Christ, and have come to a deeper love and understanding of his word.

For so large a church, a change of ministry—while being a good thing in some ways—is bound to be a critical time. You will, indeed, need to "watch and pray." I have not shrunk from passing on to you the whole counsel of God. I have sought to emphasise none other loyalty than Christ and his word. It would be foolish to imagine that *everyone* in so large a fellowship is "with me" in the strong evangelical position I have sought to maintain. Paul said, "When I am gone, grievous wolves will come in, not sparing the flock." I do not think for one moment that any grievous wolves will come in, but I do know that Satan is not and never will be converted. When I leave, he will do all in his power—masquerading as an angel of light – to compromise the message and the stand we have taken as a people and pastor these past fourteen years. He knows how to flatter with words such as *liberal, broad-minded, ecumenical, charitable* and so on.

We are living in the "last days"—days of lawlessness in the world and apostasy in Christendom. "Continue in the things which you have learned and been assured of" (2 Tim. 3:14). "Watch and pray."

The church worshipping at Melbourne Hall will ever hold a warm place in our hearts and in our prayers.
The grace of the Lord Jesus Christ be with you all,

Affectionately yours in Christ,
W Leslie Land.

One wonders, of course, why he had come to this position. He was only 58 years of age. He makes no mention of having been called to another church, and after leaving Melbourne

Hall he did not take up any ministry or permanent employment.

The letter offers possible hints, and we know that there were two periods during his ministry when he was obliged to take time away. His remarks about not everyone being with him may well have had a measure of understatement—he was not one to shout such matters from the rooftops.

By the standards and expectations of pastors sixty years or more later, his workload was intensely heavy. At no time was there a shared ministry, and men within the eldership were not expected to occupy the pulpit. The invitations to speak elsewhere, at both weekends and mid-week, were incessant, and he mentions this as a contributing factor. However, it is not clear that he undertook any greater subsequent role in that regard, and in one particular case it seems that he was not invited to preach hereafter.

It is not known when he first became aware of the first signs of what would prove a serious degenerative illness.

Five years prior to this he had printed part of a letter he had received from someone who was leaving Leicester, which could stand as the testimony of almost innumerable others:

> Continually I am discovering fresh things within, which need to be handed to Him, and frequently it has been in Melbourne Hall where God has chosen to speak. It has become a veritable spiritual home for me! ... Thank you most of all, Mr Land, for preaching Christ ... I shall continue to pray for Melbourne Hall, that God will continue to use His people there.[44]

---

[44] *Melbourne Hall Magazine* (May 1956): 382.

His departure seems almost hasty. He preached the message titled "Hegemony" from the opening words of Luke 3 and included it, as we have seen, in the January 1962 issue as his final word. Less than five weeks after penning the letter above, he wrote a final note to the church that had been his life. He offered thanks to various groups in the church. He was presented with a pastel portrait by The Young People's Fellowship, and farewell gifts from the church. He thanked the church officers, in perhaps understated words, "for the measure of love and loyalty you have shown and extended to me." Forty-three days after his announcement from the pulpit, he was no longer the minister of Melbourne Hall:

> God has sought and saved many souls (I must have baptized several hundred). Some have been thrust out into the foreign field of service ... But there is still much to be done—very much land to be possessed. The enemy is active and cunning; the days are perilous; our church is large, and a large church is fraught with difficulties as well as blessings ... You will ever be remembered in our prayers.[45]

---

[45] *Melbourne Hall Magazine* (January 1962): 329.

WORK

Declaring the Gospel

The four examples of Leslie Land's evangelistic preaching included here span the whole of his ministry. "Trust in the Lord" is a fine example of his preaching as both incisive yet simple and warm. He gave the message early in 1960. It is worth a reminder, in the context of what he says in this sermon, that at some time around this period or very shortly after, he may have had the first intimations of the illness that was to debilitate and wear him for the remaining years of his life. He rarely used alliterative headings, though readers can readily sense the "rhythm" that marks the way he explained and applied the text.

Several of the pieces were first given during 1956. This was the case with the powerful exhortation to "Remember Lot's Wife," and "The Mystery of Christ." The message from John 3:6 was given at the annual Band of Hope meeting in October 1947 five months after his arrival.

Two other messages not included here—"The Story of the Cross" and "God's Forgiveness"—were produced by Leslie Land as pamphlets, which indicates the level of his gospel ministry.

Trust in the Lord
Proverbs 3:5–6

The book of Proverbs in God's Word is not so much intended to show us how to be saved, as it is to show us how to live when saved. It is a book of divine wisdom and instruction for living a godly life. So we find this challenging exhortation, followed by a wonderful promise: "Trust in the LORD with all your heart, and do not lean on your own understanding. In all your ways acknowledge him, and he will make straight your paths" (3:5–6).

If you and I have received Christ into our hearts by faith, we have the right to be called God's children, and God has a right to ask for the trust of his redeemed children. We learn from these verses that our trust in God must have three qualities.

Unreserved

"Trust in the Lord with all your heart." There is to be no controversy, no unwillingness in our hearts about it, no inner argument. No, "it's all very well to trust God, but…" We must truly know ourselves to be utterly incapable of ordering and securing our own happiness and good. We must gladly recognise that God, our heavenly Father, has graciously committed himself to do this, in and through his son, Jesus Christ.

We should never doubt for one moment God's wisdom to know what is best for us, or his power to accomplish it, however insuperable may seem the difficulties or obstacles in the way. Indeed, to trust him with all our hearts means to be fully persuaded that he delights to care for his children, and that his faithfulness will perform and complete all that in his grace and mercy he has undertaken to do on our behalf. In other words, we his children must put all our concerns unreservedly in his hands.

Unshared

"Do not lean on your own understanding." Our trust in God must not only be unreserved, but unshared. God demands our trust exclusively. He will not share it with another. We are not to lean to our own wisdom or depend and rely on it. As Christians we are to use our understanding to the full, but we are not to transfer to it any measure of that trust which belongs, exclusively and unshared, to God.

Most Christians will agree that there have been many things in their experience which they have desired and which, had they been granted, would have proved injurious. There have been other things which we resented, but they have been overruled for our good. It becomes very clear, then, that as God's children we should renounce all idea of planning for ourselves other than in complete dependence on God's loving wisdom and guidance. We are, indeed, to use every proper means for attaining what seems good and most desirable, but as for relying on our own devices, we should not lean on our own understanding. That is something which has God's severest disapproval and censure. "Thus says the LORD: 'Cursed is the man who trusts in man and makes flesh his strength, whose heart turns away from the LORD'" (Jer. 17:5).

Universal

"In *all* your ways acknowledge him." We are exhorted to trust our heavenly father and to believe his hand is upon us ultimately for good in *all* our ways, and not merely in what we consider to be big or important happenings, or pleasant experiences. God's word tells us that he is concerned not only about the rise and fall of empires and civilisations, but that he also cares about the falling of a sparrow to the ground.

Our heavenly father wants us to acknowledge him in all things, big events or small. Yes, even in what you or I sometimes call "casual" or "accidental." "The lot is cast into the lap, but its every decision is from the LORD" (Prov. 16:33). In everything, therefore, great or small, pleasant or painful, orderly or chancy, let us acknowledge God's loving hand upon us and commit all the issues of life to him. Let our trust be unreserved, unshared, and universal.

A Promise: "He will make straight and direct your paths"

Here indeed is a gracious promise. He, your heavenly father, who has redeemed you through his Son as such great cost, will direct your paths. He will clear the road for you.

We will experience the sweetness of this promise only as we fulfil the conditions. Hearts with a controversy against God and his dealings, whose trust in him is fitful, shared and discriminating, are restless, perplexed and unblessed hearts. To trust him implicitly is to be directed by him.

How will he direct and make straight our paths? Not by dreams or visions. We are living in the day of his Spirit. Every true child of God is indwelt by the Spirit of God. "Anyone who does not have the Spirit of Christ does not belong to him" (Rom. 8:9). One of the Holy Spirit's main activities on our behalf is to open the eyes of our understanding so that we may receive and understand God's word. The Holy Spirit uses God's word to direct our paths and clear our road. Through the word he renews our minds, our judgement and way of thinking. Hence God's word becomes a lamp to our feet and a light to our path. He that follows me, says Jesus, will not walk in darkness but will have the light of life. "It is not in man who walks to direct his steps" (Jer. 10:23). God directs the paths of his children by his Spirit, renewing our minds through belief of the truth.

Moreover, God directs our paths by his providence. He often interposes for his children in a wonderful manner, averting some evil or furthering some good. Some things that happen to us seem very grievous at the time, but he knows how to accomplish his purposes of love. "God moves in a mysterious way, his wonders to perform; he plants his footsteps in the sea and rides upon the storm."[1]

A Word of Caution

Does all this mean that we, God's children, are to do nothing but sit back and trust in the Lord? No, no! Our trust in God in no way rules out the necessity for us to labour. Indeed, we are to labour as though everything depended on our exertion, but our dependence is to rest entirely upon God.

Not only must we labour, but we must also pray. God says, "I will be enquired of for this thing" (Ezek. 36:37 KJV). Trust, unaccompanied by diligence and prayer, is arrogant presumption. Diligence and prudence are part of our Christian duty. "Trust in the LORD with all your heart, and do not lean on your own understanding. In all your ways acknowledge him, and he will make straight your paths."

---

[1] The opening verse of a hymn by William Cowper (1731–1800).

"Remember Lot's Wife"
Luke 17:32

Jesus is speaking to his disciples about his second coming to this earth. He says that the state of things out in the world when he returns will be pretty much the same as it was in the days of Noah and as it was in the days of Lot. In the days of Noah, "They were eating and drinking and marrying and being given in marriage, until the day when Noah entered the ark, and the flood came and destroyed them all" (Luke 17:27). And similarly, as it was in the days of Lot, "they were eating and drinking, buying and selling, planting and building, but on the day when Lot went out from Sodom, fire and sulphur rained from heaven and destroyed them all—so will it be on the day when the Son of Man is revealed" (Luke 17:28–30).

The story of the destruction of the city of Sodom is told in Genesis 19. Whenever I read that chapter, I am amazed at the mercy God showed to Lot and his wife and family. Through their uncle Abraham they had come to know the Lord, or at least they had every opportunity of knowing him. Lot ought never to have been in Sodom. Sodom's cup of sin was brim full. God was about to visit that city in judgement. The story is rich in contrasts: the mercy and the wrath of God; Lot's faith in God and his love of the world. It is all so true to human life. It took two angels to rescue Lot, "the Lord being merciful to him" (Gen.19:16).

Why *does* the Lord love us so and go to such lengths to rescue us when we play the fool and deserve judgement? God's command was clear and unmistakeable: "Look not behind!

113

Escape for your life!" But Lot's wife, who was "behind him, looked back, and she became a pillar of salt" (19:26).

"*Remember Lot's wife!*" says Jesus. But who wants to remember a grim story like that? Remember Abraham, yes; remember David and Jonathan, yes; remember The Battle of Britain or Dunkirk. ... but who wants to remember Lot's wife? Well, you see, the gospel is concerned with the deeper issues of life, with our personal relationships to God and our eternal destiny. The Lord Jesus is coming again in person. For the world it will be a day of judgement. But the world will be carrying on just as though Christ and his cross, and his coming and his judgement mattered little or nothing to them.

"*Remember Lot's wife!*" What should we remember about her?

She Was a Very Privileged Person

She was married to a God-fearing man. The New Testament says Lot was a "righteous man" (2 Peter 2:8). Just how much his weak will was influenced by his worldly wife, we do not know. Lot chose Sodom when all the time in his heart of hearts he really loved the Lord. No wonder Peter tells us that Lot's soul was vexed from day to day by the things he saw and heard in Sodom. Uncle Abraham's soul was not vexed like that. Anyway, Mrs Lot must have heard very much about God and God's word through her husband.

Moreover, she was very privileged by reason of her relationship (through marriage) to Abraham. The gospel and the church of Jesus Christ have their human origins in the call of Abraham. Mrs. Lot spent days, weeks, and years in the company of this man of God. What a schooling! What a privilege!

She must have met the angels as they visited Abraham. She entertained them in her own home. She must have met Melchizedek, king of Salem, who blessed Abraham and offered him bread and wine. She must have listened—in many a time in Uncle Abraham's tent to that gracious believer's recounting of the ways and the counsels of God.

But privileges alone cannot save anyone. Only the Holy Spirit can unite a soul to Christ and plant saving grace in his or her heart. You may belong to a well-known evangelical church, you may sit under a faithful bible ministry week by week, you may be the child of a manse or other godly home, and not be saved. You must not confuse privileges with salvation. Your church, your home, your parents, your Guildry or your Crusader class[1], they did not and could not die for your sins and give you eternal life. Only Christ can do that. Remember Lot's wife. She was a very privileged person, but that did not save her.

She Looked Back

By looking back, she deliberately disobeyed God's command. She had lived with the Sodomites so long that it may well be she joined with them in scoffing at the idea of God's coming in judgement. The apostle Peter tells us in his second epistle that there will be scoffers in the last days, ridiculing the very idea of Christ's coming again. Jesus says, "Remember Lot's wife!"

---

[1] The Girls' Guildry was founded in 1900 by Dr. William Francis Sommerville of Glasgow and was the first girl's uniformed organisation in Britain. In 1968, the Girl's Guildry was merged with to form the Girl's Brigade. Melbourne Hall had Girls Guildry groups for different ages. Crusaders was formed in 1900 in north London with the intention of teaching the Bible to young people who did not attend church. In 2006, the organisation became known as Urban Saints. Urban Saints is a member of the Evangelical Alliance in the UK.

How we need to get right with God while it is called "today"! When the day of Christ comes there will be no time to "look back" to see if God really meant what he said so often through the preached message, commanding all people everywhere to repent *now* and to believe on his Son, the Lord Jesus Christ.

But there is much more in this backward look. It was *a look of desiring* on the part of Lot's wife. You see, her heart was really in Sodom all the time because her treasure was there. She looked back wistfully. This woman knew quite a lot about God and his call and promise to Abraham. She knew the evangelical language. She no doubt made a profession of religion and passed outwardly for one of God's people. But her heart was in the world. She had come to love Sodom and its society, its ways, its dress, is outlook and its vanity. *That* is why she looked back with a look of desire and longing.

And Jesus says, "Remember Lot's wife!" He says it, too, in relation to his coming again. The New Testament warns us that in the last days many will be lovers of pleasure more than lovers of God (2 Tim. 3:4). And how true it is that many who have made a profession of Christ are "looking back" to the Sodom, to the world from which they have been delivered and redeemed! The first glow of conversion has faded. They seldom open their bible now, only occasionally and hurriedly from a loveless sense of duty. Any excuse serves to keep them from the means of grace. The things of this world have almost jostled Jesus and eternal things out of their thoughts. They are looking back with a look of desire and wistful longing to the world which can never satisfy their hearts. "Remember Lot's wife!"

Here is a young man or woman who has met a would-be life partner, but the latter has no place for Jesus Christ. For the present the choice seems a hard one: courtship, marriage and a home; *or* following hard after Christ! They are strongly tempted to "look back." Jesus says, "Remember Lot's wife!"

Here is another who once dedicated his or her life to God for service on the foreign mission field. But since then, more alluring prospects, worldly prospects, have come to view. They are strongly tempted to 'look back'. Jesus says, "Remember Lot's wife!" and "No one who puts his hand to the plough and looks back is fit for the kingdom of God" (Luke 9:62).

She Perished!
There is something else we do well to remember about Lot's wife. She looked back from behind her husband, and she was turned into a pillar of salt, a monument in volcanic stone to the reality of God's judgements and the sinful folly of a divided heart.

The bible has very much to say about God's righteous judgements. Jesus had quite a lot to say about hell. We do not hear much about these things in modern preaching. "Conversion without tears," "a God without wrath," "a kingdom without judgement" and "a Christ without a cross" is more the popular line of our time. But God does not need anyone to save his holy character by eliminating the doctrine of hell and judgement from his revealed truth. If you are ever tempted to think that the coming of Jesus will not *really* mean judgement for the world, "remember Lot's wife." God has no need of you or me to save *him*, but you and I desperately need him to come and save *us*. This is why he sent his Son to Calvary, that we might be "*delivered from wrath through him.*" The depth of the divine love on the cross of Christ can only be truly appreciated against the dreadful reality of the divine wrath under which every man and woman abides outside Christ: "whoever does not obey the

Son shall not see life, but the wrath of God remains on him" (John 3:36).

Lot's wife perished when God visited Sodom in judgement. "Remember Lot's wife!" "For God so loved the world, that he gave his only Son, that whoever believes in him should not perish but have eternal life" (John 3:16). "If he shrinks back, my soul has no pleasure in him. But we are not of those who shrink back and are destroyed, but of those who have faith and preserve their souls" (Heb. 10:38–39).

The Mystery of Christ

I do not know what our Queen said to Dr. Billy Graham when he lunched at Windsor Castle, except for one comment which I heard on good authority. Her Majesty remarked, "When you talk about Christ, I seem to understand you, but so often when others talk of him, I do not understand what they are talking about."[1]

Now in the New Testament we read of "the mystery of Christ" (Eph. 3:4). But this "mystery of Christ" has nothing to do with clever, complicated sermons, or elaborate ceremonial and ritual which make religion seem mysterious and irrelevant to the man in the street. That is not what Paul means when he speaks of "the mystery of Christ."

Let me remind you that these New Testament epistles are letters, and they were written in the first place to young churches, i.e. to those who were very young in the faith. They were written, not to create difficulties but to clear them up, not to pose problems but to solve them. These epistles in the bible are not theological textbooks written for just a few special students, but inspired letters written to God's children and intended to help and confirm us in our faith and daily Christian living.

---

[1] The relationship between the late Queen Elizabeth II and Dr Billy Graham is described at www.billygraham.org/story/billy-graham-and-the-queen. The occasion referred to here would have taken place in 1956, which may help place the date on this brief article. In his autobiography, *Just As I Am*, Graham wrote: "Good manners do not permit one to discuss the details of a private visit with Her Majesty, but I can say that I judge her to be a woman of rare modesty and character."

What then does the apostle mean by "the mystery of Christ"? It is very true of course, that there is a great deal of mystery surrounding the person of God and his Son Jesus Christ, mystery which will only be cleared up when we are in heaven with him. But that is not what the word "mystery' means here. This word translated "mystery" could be rendered "secret," the secret regarding Christ. But we are not to think of our usual use of this word when, for example, we say, "It is a secret, I can't tell you." No, the "secret of the gospel" or "the secret of Christ" is that wonderful content of the gospel of our salvation which God *has told* to people in his word, the bible. It is a secret or mystery in the sense that if God had not revealed it or told it to us, we would never have known. This "secret of Christ" is all about the person of the Lord Jesus Christ, and if God had not been pleased to give us this revelation we would never, could never, have guessed it or thought it out. It is a secret, then, in the sense that this wonderful thing remained hidden in the mind and heart of God until he saw fit in his love to reveal and make it known to us.

What is this secret, this mystery of Christ all about?

Well, the average unbelieving person in the world thinks they know what Christianity is all about. They have an idea, but a very incomplete one. They will tell you, "I think I know a Christian when I meet one; someone on whose word you can rely; who thinks of others before themself; someone who is kind and clean and straight and fair." True, those are characteristics which you should find in every Christian. But you will also find them in measure in some who make no profession of Christ whatsoever. Indeed, that way of approach leaves out the very heart of the matter, *viz, the secret of Christ!*

You see, there are two parts to the gospel of our salvation to be distinguished but not separated.

There is the *moral* part of the gospel. This concerns the character and the conduct which we exhibit and display day by day. This part of the gospel comes out very clearly in our Lord's teaching. Most men can appreciate this side of the gospel when it is presented to them. It somehow rings a bell in their conscience. "This is right," they say, "If only this could be carried into practice the world would be a better place." It is the ethics of Christianity.

But notice, will you, that the teaching of moral virtue is not the exclusive right or monopoly of Christianity. There are other religions and philosophies which extol moral virtue. But to the average man of the world, this aspect of the gospel is the sum total of Christianity. This is why he looks on church-going and public worship as somewhat irrelevant. After all, a man may go to church and not be a good living man. On the other hand, a man may never enter a church and yet present a very fair and commendable life before the eyes of the world.

Now this view of Christianity is all very well so far as it goes. The trouble is it does not go very far. It is a sort of worm's-eye view of the matter. It just looks at things from below. But if you read the New Testament you will have to admit that there is far more in Christianity than a moral code. The morality set forth in the New Testament is merely a part of the *fruit* of the Christian life, but it is not the *root* of the matter. The root of the matter is the person Jesus Christ himself. This is where "the mystery of Christ" comes in. It is that which God has revealed to us by his Spirit concerning the person of his Son.

Jesus Christ is not simply the founder of a religion called Christianity. He is not just one who has made an impact on the thought and life of the world and gone away leaving us to put his ideas into practice. There have been such founders of religions in the world. But the essence of Christianity *is the person of Christ himself,* he is the secret of the whole matter.

Judged by God's standard of righteousness, which is Christ, no one on earth is able to live a life pleasing to him. This is where the worm's-eye view comes so tragically short of the God's-eye view. The bible puts it this way, "The Lord looks down from heaven on the children of man, to see if there are any who understand, who seek after God. They are all turned aside; ... there is none who does good, not even one" (Ps. 14:2–3), and "all have sinned and fall short of the glory of God" (Rom. 3:23). The bible tells us that what God was doing in Christ was not simply teaching us what kind of people we ought to be, but that God was in Christ reconciling the world to himself (2 Cor. 5:19).

Here then is the root of the matter. Sin is not just something wrong which simply needs to be pointed out to us for us to put it right. Sin is a radical breach with God bringing in its train guilt, helplessness, and condemnation. Sin has made us guilty before God, but the mystery or secret of Christ is that God in his love has let his Son bear the punishment and the judgement of our sins: "He himself bore our sins in his body on the tree" (1 Peter 2:24). Sin has left us helpless and powerless, but the mystery of Christ is that "Christ may dwell in your hearts through faith;" we can be "strengthened with power through his Spirit in your inner being" (Eph. 3:16–17). Sin has alienated us from the life of God (Eph. 4:18), but the mystery of Christ is that he *is* the life (John 14:6), and when we receive Christ into our hearts by faith, we receive the gift of eternal life. "Whoever has the Son has life; whoever does not have the Son of God does not have life" (1 John 5:12). Sin has shut us out from the glory of heaven (Rev. 21:27), but the mystery of Christ is that God has opened heaven to us in his Son, "this mystery, which is Christ in you, *the hope of glory*" (Col. 1:27). Sin has broken relationships between man and man, resulting in a divided and broken world, but the mystery of Christ is that we can be *one* in Christ Jesus. God has revealed to us "the fellowship of the mystery," "to make all men see what is the fellowship of the mystery" (Eph. 3:9, KJV). Only in him are unity and lasting peace to be found, Jews and Gentiles, Israeli and Arabs, Russians and the West may come together in the person of Jesus Christ, "fellow heirs, members of the same body, and partakers of the promise in Christ Jesus through the gospel" (Eph. 3:6).

The secret of the whole matter is Christ, "Christ in you, the hope of glory." The secret of a truly vital Christian is Christ. The inner secret of the Christian life is a spiritual union with Christ. God has unveiled this lovely inner secret of the gospel of our salvation in his word, and he will make his Son to mean everything to you when you are ready to acknowledge your sinnership, to break with sin and let Christ into your heart.

"That which is born of the flesh is flesh, and that which is born of the Spirit is spirit"[1]
John 3:6

I have to confess that when the General Secretary of the County Band of Hope Union called on me some time ago, I did my best to decline this invitation and honour conferred upon me tonight. I have never signed the "Pledge"! I told him so, but the more I protested, the more convinced he seemed to become that the Centenary should be celebrated at Melbourne Hall, myself being the preacher. Let me say here, if signing a pledge helps *you*, or *would* help you to live a better life, then in God's name sign it, my friend.

I am one of those who need something more than a pledge of my own undertaking. The message I bring you tonight concerns that "something more"; and if it finds a place in your heart and home, then, as far as you and I are concerned, the brewers and publicans will just have to close down; not because they cannot get the stuff to sell, but because they cannot ever *give* it away.

I am often interested in the many drinking slogans and adverts of our day. The popular slogan "Beer is best" will do by way of illustration. You may think I am going to tear that slogan and the rest of them to shreds, go on to expound a few scientific principles, recite some physiological consequences,

---

[1] This sermon was preached on Sunday evening, 19 October, on the occasion of the celebration of the Centenary of the National Band of Hope Union. The Band of Hope was the public face of the Temperance Movement. Today in Britain it is Hope UK.

economic statistics, add a few harrowing anecdotes, and then go away fondly hoping I have made you all into total abstainers. I am not going to do anything of the kind.

We will let the slogan stand, for it well placards a certain level or kind of life about which I want to speak plainly. I am not concerned merely with the "alcoholic," the poor man or woman in the grip of that awful disease. I am not concerned only with men and women who, otherwise gifted and talented, are sapping and destroying their mental powers and prospects with this accursed habit. Nor am I thinking only of broken, ruined homes and marriages, or of the crime of cultivating acres for brewing purposes when nations, women and children are perishing for want of wheat and bread. No, I am thinking rather of a level of life which is the best that multitudes of our fellow men and women know, a life roofed in by *this* world, a life which misses the goal and purpose for which Almighty God created humanity, a life which ends, like the book of Genesis, "in a coffin in Egypt." I never see these drink slogans and adverts but what I feel that any one of them would make a good label, not only for the bottle, but for the outlook, the mentality, the level of life which keeps the drink traffic alive.

There was once a gentleman who sought an interview with Jesus, by night, a cultured man. I'm sure you would have liked him. Any prosperous business firm might have thought him quite a catch as their chairman. You would never have found him involved in any scandal. You would never have found him "under the table" after a dinner party. He opened his interview with Jesus with some sincere and lofty sentiments. And what do you think Jesus said to him? He said, "Nicodemus, you must be born from above." This didn't make sense to Nicodemus: "How can a man be born when he is old?" Jesus said to him:

"That which is born of the flesh is flesh, and that which is born of the Spirit is spirit. Do not wonder at me telling you, 'You must all be born from above.'"

The bible, of course, isn't a textbook of science, but it has a knack of wrapping a lot of truth up in a very small parcel. In the early Genesis creation story, we come across the simple phrase "after its kind" ten times. "After its kind." How true of our natural, human birth. That which is born of the flesh is flesh. We don't slide, we don't "evolve" into the Kingdom of God. What is born of the flesh is flesh, and by "flesh" the New Testament doesn't just mean the physical substance of our bodies, but the whole natural man, with his sin-marred personality, desires, appetites and cravings—his "beer is best" outlook, his "I want to be happy" philosophy of life.

The fact that the brewers *know* that they can get a response by placarding such slogans as "Beer is best," that the comedians *know* they can draw applause and provide mass entertainment by "drinking jokes," that so much time, space and money can be allocated to this traffic even during a national "crisis," are palpable testimony to the truth of this divine pronouncement, "That which is born of the flesh is flesh."

Huxley used to say that between the highest brute beast and the lowest man there is a divergence "almost infinite."[2] Between the realm of the flesh (with its "beer is best" outlook) and the realm of the Spirit (with its God-centred outlook) there is a bottomless gulf, a "divergence almost infinite." Sin has opened that gulf. The bridging of it is a task for God, and he has done it. He has done it in Jesus Christ. He has come over to our side of the gulf in order that he might lift us over, as it

---

[2] Although this presumably would have been Thomas Huxley (1825–1895), I have not been able to trace the exact quotation.

were, to *his* side. But even God cannot lift *sinners* over unless he first does something about our sin. Otherwise he would not be God! He *has* done something about our sin. He has taken it out of the way forever. As Brunner puts it,[3] sin is no mere error, no mere aberration or moral delinquency, "Sin is a real obstacle between man and God," and the one Mediator between God and man, the man Jesus Christ, has dealt with it: "He bore our sins in his own body on the tree."

"I cannot understand it," you say. You would be God if you could. But you may experience it. It is the first wonder of a miracle called "Salvation." Forgiven for Christ's sake. The second wonder of this miracle is that God plants part of his very own life and nature in the forgiven human heart and personality. There it is, a miracle, a "birth from above," eternal life. It begins to pulsate and to cry out "*Abba, Father!*" It begins to get into a person's thinking, into their looking, speaking, wishing, marrying—into their very nature. Old appetites, cravings and thirstings begin to fall away as dead desires. A new love, a new life begins to possess their heart and personality, taking them captive, body, soul and spirit. The "beer is best" outlook on life now shrivels and fades. "Christ is better"? No, he is beyond compare. Christ is all in all and "for me to live is Christ!" If you would have this new life tonight, you may do so, not by any act of "self-reformation," but by receiving the Lord Jesus Christ as your Saviour and your daily friend. That which is born of the flesh is flesh, and that which is born of the Spirit is Spirit; and the fruit of the Spirit is love, joy, peace, long-suffering, gentleness, goodness, faith, meekness, temperance. Against such there is no law.

---

[3] Emil Brunner (1889–1966) was a Swiss neo-Orthodox theologian.

Faith and Life

Leslie Land's teaching and preaching regarding the Christian life intertwined life and faith. He was never fearful of speaking of "doctrine." We find him saying, for example,

> God does not need anyone to save his holy character by eliminating the doctrine of hell and judgement from his revealed truth.

> The only apostolic succession that matters is that we should continue steadfastly in the apostle's doctrine; that we should love, adore and proclaim the same Saviour and be indwelt by the same Holy Spirit.

Quoting those who say "We must tell people what God has *done* rather than give them doctrine," his rejoinder is "now that is a dangerous line of reasoning. True, our salvation does rest in what God has done for us in the person of his Son. But it rests equally in what God has *said* in his Word."

Yet he also cautions. God "doesn't just fill your head with evangelical doctrines. You may know all doctrine and not be saved." Speaking to those who would preach he warns "always teach and preach Jesus Christ. But avoid specialising in any particular doctrine."

We find this biblical blend in these next seven messages. His brief new year greeting in 1949 on departing by another way exemplifies the challenging and unexpected ways he applied Scripture. "The New Look" was given in May 1948. The most complete statement he gave of his position on what we may call the doctrines of grace was given over two issues of the magazine in 1955, reproduced here under the general title of "Conversion." He had touched on these themes in a message not included in this book, on "The Family Likeness" given in October 1952.

"The Earnest of our Inheritance" is a brief but lucidly helpful explanation and application of the verse in Ephesians 1, given early in 1950. Land almost always chose one of his Sunday sermons to write for the magazine. The final inclusion in this section is not taken from the magazine but is the closing study he gave as part of the Bible School series on the final appearing of Jesus. It focuses mainly on the theme of "loving his appearing" and has helpful examples of Land's ways of illustrating his messages, often making evident his readiness to confess his own perceived limited understanding.

A.D. 1949
A Happy New Year!

"Peace I leave with you; my peace I give to you. Not as the
world gives do I give to you. Let not your hearts be troubled,
neither let them be afraid."
John 14:27

"They departed to their own country by another way."
Matthew 2:12

These wise men had been to Bethlehem. They had been di-
vinely led there. They had seen Jesus, the holy child, the new
born king, and they departed into their own country another
way. They could not return to Herod, not after seeing the
Christ. *We* have been to Bethlehem. We have seen Jesus. Grace
led us to him. We have seen the manger, the cross, the empty
tomb; we have caught the meaning of the advent; we have
heard for ourselves the glad tidings of good news; we have had
an encounter with the God-Saviour.

We must return to "our own country." We must return to
the humdrum and toil of everyday life, but we must surely return "another way." We cannot, we simply cannot return to
Herod, to the life that slays and crucifies the Son of God afresh.
We who have found reconciliation and peace in the Lord Jesus
Christ, we cannot, we simply cannot go back to the old life, the
old ways, the old sins. Our feet shall journey another way, for
we have found the Saviour who is Christ the Lord!

Leslie Land

Come, let us anew our journey pursue,
Roll round with the year,
And never stand still till the Master appear,
His adorable will let us gladly fulfill,
And our talents improve,
By the patience of hope, and the labour of love.
Oh, that each in the day of his coming may say,
"I have fought my way through;
I have finished the work thou didst give me to do!'
Oh, that each from his Lord may receive the glad word,
"Well and faithfully done!
Enter into my joy, and sit down on my throne!"[1]

---

[1] This largely unknown hymn is by Charles Wesley. It was first published as the fifth hymn in his collection *Hymns for New Year's Day,* 1750.

The New Look

"Those who look to him are radiant."
Psalm 34:5

I was travelling in a train from Waterloo the other day. Just before we left London, four people got into our carriage, a lady and three Chinese men. Their look attracted our attention. I said to my wife, "Those men are Christians" How did I know? I knew by their faces. I had nothing more to go upon than their look. Some folks imagine that we are all Christians nowadays, but that, unhappily, just isn't true. It is shallow nonsense. We are *not* all Christians. There are plenty of men and women who are outwardly and seemingly honest, decent and straightforward, yet they are not Christians. But those three men from China, and the lady with them, had a look, a light about their faces which told me that they were Christians, that is, believers on the Lord Jesus Christ. No, I do not mean that they wore a permanent grin or a sickly smile. They were perfectly natural, and yet all the changing expressions on their faces somehow or other never seemed to obliterate a shine, a light, a look which comes from knowing and living close to Christ.

We are hearing quite a lot today about the "new look." It is nothing more than a passing mode of fashion, something which ladies can acquire if they possess the money and the coupons.[1] I hear the men are getting it too! It is "*new*" only in the sense that it has not been "worn" recently. It is bound to

---

[1] Clothing rationing had been introduced in the UK on 1 June 1941. Rationing continued until 1949.

133

become old and pass away again. But the *new* look we are more interested in comes from *within* a person. You need neither money nor coupons to get it. It never becomes dated. It always *has* been the new look all down history; new in the sense of coming from *outside* this world, and from a sphere, a Person, over and above the changing forms and fashions of this world.

But some may ask: "Is it *real*? Is it *practical*? How do you get it?" Now, when you use the words "real" and "practical," you are heading for difficulty and trouble with some people. "Real" and "practical" to them relate merely to the five senses. Food, drink, clothes and money are real and practical. Religion, the things of the spirit, they are unreal, unpractical, extras, a trifle unnecessary. Sadly enough, it is possible to go on in this animalistic state and even be proud of it, allowing *means* to an end to become the end itself. Food, drink, clothes and money are means to an end in life. But the "new look' we are thinking about just now is a sign, a hallmark on a person's face that their inner life and personality have already begun to realise and experience the end for which they were created, namely, "to glorify God and to enjoy him forever." This new look on a Christian disciple's face is something of the purpose of God, the grace of God, shining through.

Have you ever heard it said that two people who are in love and live together for long, tend to become like each other in looks? I think there may be something in it. But this I know, when a man or a woman is brought into fellowship with God in Jesus Christ that man or woman slowly but surely gets something of the Christ look in their face, and of the God-look about them. They may not be what the world calls beautiful or handsome. Those four folks in the train were not beautiful or handsome in any worldly sense, but I tell you there was a light, a radiance about their countenances which was a spiritual delight to look upon. Where did it come from? Well, you know, it's possible to *play* at being Christians (taking great care never to go too far); but then, again, it's possible to touch the real thing.

Have you ever looked down in your garden at some shapeless, lifeless, motionless thing, and then, all at once, it *moves*. Your face changes as you exclaim, "It's alive!" Well, it's possible to go on for years toying with a dead religion, a creed, a code of ethics, and then, all at once one day, to meet Christ. "It's alive!" "*He's* alive!" Anything may happen! Something *will* happen when you and I encounter the living Christ. Whether lovers as they walk and talk together ever really become like each other, I don't know. Whether a husband and wife, as they sit in silent companionship on either side of the fireplace, ever become like each other, I am not sure. But one thing I know, as a sinner and his new-found Saviour walk and talk together day by day, there steals a likeness, a Christlikeness, into the heart and into the look of that saved sinner, for you can't commune with Jesus and not get more like him, and the eventide of life will surely only find us *more* like this wonderful, transforming, transfiguring Saviour. The greying hair may to the world speak of an end, but the "new look" on an aged pilgrim's face speaks of Christ, whom to know is life eternal, and of a new creation in him.

Sin has broken our relationship with God. It has blighted and marred the image and likeness of God throughout our moral being. And even on our faces godlessness and the fruits of our human godlessness—pride, arrogance, selfishness, lust and vice—reveal themselves in men and women. But the Lord Jesus has brought us back again to God, has brought God back again to you and to me. The Psalmist says, "Those who look to him are radiant." This transforming miracle has been going on all down the ages. Who looked?[2] Who were lightened? He doesn't say. He simply says, "they looked." Does he mean Abraham? Yes, I'm sure Abraham got the new look when he decided to cut with Ur of the Chaldees and go God's way. Jesus said, "Your father Abraham rejoiced that he would see my day. He saw it and was glad" (John 8:56). Yes, Abraham had the light of Christ in his eyes. And Isaac, the child of promise, I am sure he *got* the new look as he communed with God out in the fields morning and evening. They looked unto him and were lightened.

Also, do you remember when Moses came down from the Mount of communion with God, we read 'Moses did not know that the skin of his face shone' (Ex. 34.29). He didn't know that his face was aglow after speaking with God. Yes, speaking with God, that is the secret. Leaping the centuries, we recall that Stephen the Martyr, also got that new look. Those who were about to murder him looked upon him and were nonplussed to find that his face shone with a heavenly light. They had accused Stephen of speaking against Moses, and now the same light which had been seen on the face of Moses millennia before, shone on Stephen's face.

The Psalmist doesn't say *who* looked. Just "they," ordinary sinful men and women, who all down the ages, have been looking to him and have been lightened. Those people in the train, yes, they had looked. I *knew* they had, and when I reached the end of my journey, I happened to overhear the lady mentioned her father's name. It was the name of a well-known man of

---

[2] He was quoting from the King James Version of the Bible, where Psalms 34:5 says, "They looked unto Him and were lightened.'

God. Yes, these folk had the light of Christ upon their faces because they had Jesus Christ in their hearts.

There is something else about this new look which Jesus brings. It doesn't stop at a shining countenance. Christ brings not only a new look, but a new way of looking at other men and women. For one thing, I believe those three Chinese men in the train looked differently on that woman who travelled with them and who was evidently their teacher and guide. Yes, Christ in the heart can help a man to look on a woman differently. I do not believe that conversion renders any man unnatural or unsexed. No, rather, I believe that all our gifts and capacities are hallowed and controlled when we let Jesus Christ have the Lordship of our lives. Human love, human relationships, human laughter are all enriched and enhanced when Christ is in them, and "something lives in every hue Christless eyes have never seen."[3]

Christ changes our looking on all our fellow men and women. That crowd at the football match, that queue waiting for the bus, this congregation here in church, all consist of men and women for whom Christ died. The new look sees them all as potential brothers and sisters in Christ. The new look sees that one thing matters more than anything else, namely that they should all become the children of God by receiving Jesus Christ. Do *you* look on men and women like that? On your neighbours? On that difficult person with whom your life is bound up? If this new look is not terribly practical, what *is*? This new look, this new way of looking, has the power to change all our human relationships, power to change the face of the world. It sees all our human unrest, all the ugliness and wretchedness and misery of our world as the outcome of a

---

[3] George W. Robinson (1838–1877), "Loved with everlasting love."

broken relationship with God, and it knows where mercy and healing and reconciliation are to be found, and it looks on men and women with the Saviour's Calvary love glowing in the heart.

I must add one thing more about this new look. It knows how to look out on the future and yet still experience peace and certainty in the heart. Can you do *that*? The man with the new look has his whole future vested in Jesus Christ. It was just the same with Abraham and with all the saints of old. They were never indifferent to this world, but they knew how to "travel light," to hold loosely by the things of time. They were seeking a better country, a "heavenly." They were looking for a city which has foundations. God's people were never *uninterested* in what Egypt would do, in what Assyria, Babylon, Greece or Rome would do. We are by no means uninterested today in what Russia will do, or what America will do. In fact, the man and woman in Christ is more intelligently interested in world affairs than the man and woman who is outside Jesus Christ. But there is a vast difference, because our trust, our sure and certain hope, is in Jesus Christ.

How do you get this new look, this new looking, this new outlook? Not by looking at yourself. Not by looking at other Christians. No, you get the new look by looking away to Jesus Christ. But how do you look to Jesus Christ? How do you look to *anyone* who can help you? Why, you just *trust* them, you commit yourself to them, you take them at their word. Do that now with the Lord Jesus if you have never done so before. *You* need a Saviour, a Saviour from sin, just as *I* do. Jesus is that! By the Cross of Calvary he is God's perfect and *only* provision for our salvation. Look to him! Behold the Lamb of God who bears away the sin of the world! *You* need a Saviour, just as *I* do, not only from sin, but from the love of sinning, from the frustration, the emptiness, the meaninglessness of life. The risen Christ is that Saviour. Look to him now. Jesus says, I came that they may have *life*, I came that your joy may be full. It's not for angels, but for sinful men. It's not a mere *feeling*, it's a *fact*. Stake all upon it, upon him. "Those who look to him are radiant."

> I heard the voice of Jesus say,
> "I am this dark world's light;
> Look unto me, your morn shall rise,
> And all your day be bright."

> I looked to Jesus, and I found
> in him, my star, my sun;
> And in that light of life I'll walk
> Till travelling days are done.[4]

---

[4] Horatius Bonar (1808–1889), "I heard the voice of Jesus say."

Conversion

The Lord Jesus is speaking. He says, "No one can come to me unless the Father who sent me draws him. And I will raise him up on the last day … This is why I told you that no one can come to me unless it is granted him by the Father" (John 6:44–65).

Conversion is in the air and we thank God for it.[1] There is a return to the theme, to the desire for conversion in many churches and in Christian circles. People are talking about conversion, about those who are being "converted.' I want us to think about conversion, reverently, from the *Godward* side. It is a great mystery, but because so much has been revealed in God's word, I need not apologise for seeking to open it up. Later we will look at it from the *manward* side. It takes place in the human heart, but I want us to look at it first from God's side, from the side of Heaven.

The Godward Side

In seeking to understand conversion you and I are apt to think simply of what goes on in the heart. It is very natural that we should. But as I read my Bible, I am convinced that when a soul is converted, more goes on in Heaven than in our heart. All Heaven—the whole Godhead—is involved in the conversion of a sinner to Christ.

---

[1] Billy Graham (1918–2018) was preaching in Glasgow during a six-week All Scotland Crusade from March 21 to April 30, 1955. Some estimates of total audiences were as high as 2.5 million people.

It happens to be Trinity Sunday,[2] and I find myself thinking about God the Father, God the Son, and God the Holy Spirit. I am not going to explain them. I cannot. I am just inviting you to meditate with me about the working of God the Father, God the Son and God the Holy Spirit in the conversion of a sinner to Jesus Christ.

The text reveals to us that when a soul is converted Christ is the object of its faith. "They came to me," says Jesus. It is always to him. But the text also reveals clearly that God the Father, gives his consent. He concurs in this tremendous event. "No one can come to me," says Jesus, "unless the Father who sent me draws him." Later on, when some of his listeners were finding some of his statements very hard to understand. He says, "Well, I said to you a little while ago that no one can come to Me unless the Father draws him."

So we are on the Godward side of the mystery. Already we are out of our depth, but reverently we will go on, because if God has revealed something about this mystery then we do well to pay heed to it. Otherwise our conception, our understanding of conversion will be a very earthly one, and we will do insult to God and to this miracle. Not only does the Father concur and conspire and consent, but the Lord Jesus also consents. He says "All that the Father gives me will come to me, and whoever comes to me I will never cast out" (John 6:37). "I will receive him." The Father gives, the Father draws, the Son receives and then in this same chapter the Lord Jesus says it is the Holy Spirit who gives life (v. 63).

When you look at the sky on an evening, it isn't often that you see a coming together of the heavenly bodies, a conjunction of the planets. I am not an astronomer, but I believe that

---

[2] Trinity Sunday fell on June 5 in 1955.

there have not been many conjunctions of the planets. It is a rare occurrence. In the Heaven of Heavens and the word of God we have a conjunction of God the Father, God the Son and God the Holy Spirit. At Jesus' birth, his baptism and at our redemption on Calvary God the Father, Son and Holy Spirit were all working together for the new creation of souls that are dead in sin.

They are again at work every time a sinner is drawn to Christ. We find the Father giving the soul to Jesus. Jesus said, "Father, they were yours and you gave them to me." We were given to Christ from everlasting. We were chosen in him before the foundation of the world. The Bible reveals that on the cross of Calvary there is a sense in which we were with Christ—a great *rendezvous* of all the redeemed, out of every age, every kindred, were there on the cross. He bore our sins in his body on the Tree, and if he bore our sins, he bore our persons. We were with him, on the Godward side.

You say, "Oh, I wasn't born yet. I hadn't come into this world." No, but you were in the plan, you were in the heart of God, and you were given to Christ. And there comes a moment in time when Christ comes into possession of the soul which was given to him. Something happens in church under the preaching of the word. Sometimes it happens in the home, when the soul is bowed, perhaps by the bedside, in repentance and broken in heart and spirit. It is as though the Father says to the Son, "Son, there is that soul I gave you. I am about to draw her, draw him to you. Go and possess them! Go and dwell in their heart for ever." God the Father gives us to his Son at our conversion. He woos us, draws us. He makes Christ more desirable than anything or anyone besides. He makes him irresistible in that moment, and he comes and dwells in our hearts by faith. He receives us.

He is waiting to receive some this very day, who are going to be drawn to him. The bible says that the Son is sitting in heaven, waiting and expecting, till all his enemies are made his footstool. Before that day he also is waiting for those who are his to be drawn by the cords of love, by the Father to the Son. They have been given to him by way of reward, by way of charge, to redeem, to cleanse and to lead to glory, and he is waiting. I don't know who they are today, but they are going to be drawn to Christ, by God the Father, and Jesus will receive and apprehend them. This is how Paul puts it. "Why," he says, "Before I apprehended Christ, he apprehended me. He laid hold upon me, laid his hand on my life. And I am pressing on to take hold of that for which Christ Jesus took hold of me" (Phil. 3:12).

At the hour of your conversion, you were taken hold of by Christ, you were embraced by God the Son, and God the Holy Spirit was sent into your heart. "Because you are sons, God has sent the Spirit of his Son into our hearts, crying, 'Abba! Father!', dear Father" (Gal. 4:6). It isn't only that the Spirit of God is sent into your heart, so that you begin to love God, to talk to him as a child talks to its father, and to call God *your* Father with meaning. The Holy Spirit also creates in us what the bible calls a new creature. "If anyone is in Christ, he is a new creation. The old has passed away; behold, the new has come" (2 Cor. 5:17). Remember that although I am daring to speak of tremendous things in human language, the realities of which I speak do not mean *less* than the language I use. I am limited because I have only human language in which to say them, but the realities themselves transcend all that I can express or think.

The old person had eyes and ears, hands and feet. Spiritually speaking the new man who now has come to birth has eyes, through which he or she looks on Christ, as never having seen him before. He has heard him preached, but now he sees the Son, sees him with an eye that was blind before to Christ. Believers know what it is to eye Christ. You have seen Jesus and it is the most wonderful sight, compared with which all the sights in the world now take a very second place.

Also, the Holy Spirit has given you ears, and you hear the word of God. Oh, you have heard a minister preaching, you have heard the hymns, you have had religion perhaps for years, but when conversion is real, when it is an act of God the Father, Son and Holy Spirit and does not rest in human persuasion, then the Holy Spirit gives new ears to hear the deep things of God. And how you love to hear them. He gives new hands to take hold of Christ. New feet to come to Christ. A new appetite. The natural man cannot make sense of it, that you could ever want to gather around the word of God! It does not make sense to him.

New Testament Examples

All this is not just doctrine. You find it illustrated in the New Testament. There was Saul, a rebel, a chief of sinners, a persecutor, a blasphemer. He had no leanings towards Christ. But he says, "There came a time when it pleased God to do something. Before that time I was just like any other Jew. I was without Christ. But there came a time when it pleased God to reveal his son in me." On the Damascus Road the second person of the Trinity came in. He said "Saul, Saul!" He knew him by name. He met Christ who laid his hand on him. Then through Ananias God sent the Spirit into his heart and Saul's heart became aflame with the love and glory of Christ. That is conversion.

It happened also to Cornelius, the centurion, in Caesarea. God moved first and took the initiative. "Cornelius," he said, "send down to Joppa; I have a servant there named Peter. He will come and tell you about my Son. He will draw you to my Son." Father, Son and Holy Spirit all came together and operated in the heart and life of Cornelius, and he was a saved man. That is conversion.

God is speaking to us from this mysterious side of conversion. We learn first that God is telling us that conversion is not a light thing. All heaven is engaged in it. Even the angels are stirred (Luke 15:10). There is a stir on earth too. Those at home sometimes think we are mad. Those in the workplace, those in the college, the school, the hospital. Sometimes they are amazed. Sometimes they mock. "These men are full of new wine!" "No," says Peter, "This is an act of God, when a soul is really born again." Don't take a light view of conversion.

Second, we learn that if anyone is in doubt as to whether you are born again, wait upon God. I beg you to give heed to his word, to attend to the means of grace, that you may be ready in that supreme moment when God the Father, having given you his Son, draws you to the Son. When the Son receives you and sends the Holy Spirit into your heart and you find yourself crying "Abba, Father—dear Father," and you belong to him, for time and eternity.

Third, I would remind myself and all Christian workers to get a right view of this matter, to remember what your part is and what your part is *not*. Only God can save a soul, and God the Father, Son and Holy Spirit are involved in it, more concerned than you ever could be. You are called to be his witnesses, to say what you know of him. Don't talk about what you don't know—it doesn't ring true. Say what you know of this Christ. Don't recite things you don't know.

Be a witness to him, if you can witness. God has called us to witness and pray. If we spent more time in prayer and less in anxious talk about how to get conversions, there would be more people converted. Talk less about it and pray more for it. God has been pleased to use the instrument of prayer and intercession. I think of a mother who prayed thirteen years for her son centuries ago. She went on praying all those years, and Augustine was born again by God the Father, Son and Holy Spirit. And what a man God chose! I have often said, and I say it again, I had a mother whose exhortations and rebukes cut little or no ice with me, but her prayers got me down. She prayed for me, and God drew me to his Son and gave me his Holy Spirit, so that I longed to preach Christ to others and witness to him.

When the real thing happens all the glory must go to God. You were only a witness, only an intercessor. You were only an example of what grace can do in a saved soul.

The Human Side

What does God do in the human heart in bringing someone to Christ? God draws a soul to Jesus Christ by teaching that person concerning his Son. He woos the sinner through the record in his Word, through the witness and testimony that God has given about his Son. First, what is it that God the Father teaches you and me about his Son, to draw us to him? Second, how does he do it?

What Does God Teach About His Son?

What is "the testimony that God has borne concerning his Son" (1 John 5:10)? John briefly and tersely sums up God's record in this way. "This is the testimony, that God gave us eternal life, and this life is in his Son. Whoever has the Son has life; whoever does not have the Son of God does not have life" (1 John 5:11–12). John goes on to make it clear that he is writing these things for a double reason. First, so that those who are Christians might be assured that they have eternal love. But it is not only written for those who already are believing on Jesus the Son. It is also plain from the context that these things have been written for the sake of those who, up to now, have resisted and do not believe. He writes so that they might believe that Jesus is the Son of God, that they, that we, may be drawn to Christ.

I cannot do it. I am not going to persuade you to be a Christian by eloquence, by rhetoric or logic of my own. I am here to be a witness and to preach the gospel, the everlasting gospel of God's Son. God must supply the power. Will you be ready?

There are two great pronouncements in God's record. First, that God has given us eternal life. Second, that this life is to be had in his Son.

God Has Given Us Eternal Life

Eternal life is to be had today. God has made it available! When John says God gave "us" eternal life, he is not thinking only of a body of believers who have already received it. "Us" is general. Imagine, by way of illustration, that someone left a large legacy to your church to be used for sending people to work in mission situations. That does not mean that everyone will actually benefit, that everyone in your church will apply for part of that legacy. So it is with the gospel. There with no need for anyone to perish, or to go on in unbelief and frustration, disillusion and despair. For this is God's record, that he has given us eternal life and you may have it in and through Jesus Christ.

Eternal life differs altogether from the life we have by natural birth. Eternal life is life that is right and at peace with God. It is "God-life,' fulness of life and unending life. It is a life that will come to its own, to maturity and perfection, when we go to be with him. You cannot earn it, you cannot buy it, you cannot merit it by saying "Well, I will live the best kind of life I know, and then hope that God will give it to me." It isn't to be had on those terms. The gift of God is eternal life through Jesus Christ (Rom. 6:23).

This Life Is to Be Had in His Son

"Whoever has the Son has life; whoever does not have the Son of God does not have life." God's word says that if you reject that statement you make God a liar (1 John 5:10). In the New Testament you will seldom find that God speaks verbally and audibly, and when he does it is always concerning his Son. With the closing of these New Testament times God no longer chooses to speak audibly and vocally, for we have the testimony and record concerning his Son. He speaks through that record. He will speak to a human soul silently. What does he say? He always says, "Go to my Son. If you want eternal life, go to my Son." The words may vary but he always says, "I can't give you eternal life outside my Son."

You ask "Why?" "Well," he says, "My Son gave his flesh for the life of the world. My Son went to the cross for you when he was here on earth, and you can have life no other way." It is at the cross that sin is put away, that the broken relationship is healed, that the life of God can come in.

> Go to my Son. This is my beloved Son, hear him. I have no other word to say to you. I have spoken my last word in grace. One day I will speak again in judgement, but go to my Son while it is called "Today," because there is no judgment or condemnation to those who are in my Son. There is no-one else in heaven or on earth who can give you life.

Yet Jesus says to those around him, "You won't come, that you might have life." If someone who is without this life reads these words, whatever your background may be, whatever race or nationality, come to him today. He was wounded for your transgressions; he was crushed for your iniquities; the punishment which has secured your peace was laid on him and through those wounds you may be healed (Isa. 53:5).

Notice it is he who has the *Son.* You cannot just go directly to God for pardon. You cannot go to God and say "Oh God, bless me! I want your blessing. Give me your righteousness." He says, "Receive my Son." All that God has for you is mediated through the Son. Not only pardon, but eternal life and heaven itself. He does not expect you to understand all this at conversion. The person then is simply troubled with sin and how to get peace with God and comes to Christ for pardon and reconciliation. But if your conversion is really of God, and not in your own power, he will draw your soul nearer and nearer to Christ. Jesus will become more wonderful to you, and he will kindle a fire of love "on the mean altar of your heart."[3]

---

[3] He is referring to a line from Charles Wesley's hymn, "O Thou who camest from above."

How Does God Do This?

How does the Father teach you and me so that we may have eternal life in his Son? Let me say how he does not do it. He doesn't just fill your head with evangelical doctrines. You may know all doctrine and not be saved. If you give diligent attention to the Scriptures you can learn quite a lot. If you sit under a faithful ministry week by week you also will learn much, and you should do. You may know a tremendous amount about Christ and have it all cut and dried and pigeon-holed, and be able to argue eloquently and even to preach, yet not have life.

What does the Father do? I don't know whether I can put it into words, it is so wonderful. The Father takes one truth, it may be just one, that the preacher has uttered concerning his Son, and he takes it right home to your soul in a way that he has never done before. Out of all the things that the preacher might say about Christ Jesus there is just one thing, one pearl about Christ, and the Father takes it right home and penetrates your soul. You may have heard a lot of sermons. You may have heard Billy Graham time and again. You have heard me and heard others. You have read books and read your Bible—and you are still without life. Somehow the Father has not yet drawn you to his Son. I cannot explain it. It will be like a beam of light going down into the darkness. It will be as though Jesus Christ steps out of the printed page, out of the spoken sermon, and you will say

> I have met him—today! I have heard no end about him. I am well up in doctrine and I can argue and converse freely, but today I have met him. He is real. He is my Saviour, my Christ. I have been on the Emmaus Road today. My heart burned within me as he spoke with me by the way. I thought I had life because I belonged to such and

such a church or chapel. I thought I had life because I was a deacon, or a Sunday School teacher, and belonged to such and such religious organisation. But today I heard the Father speaking to me, and he told me that this life is not to be had in this or that, but in his Son.

How Will I Know?

You say, "How will I know?" If your conversion is real—if it is in the power of God and the Father really has spoken to your soul—then you will be in love with Christ. Though you may not understand what is going on at that moment, your heart will be suddenly warmed within you towards Christ. Christ will speak out of the printed page and be a real presence to you, more real than the person sitting next to you.

You will instinctively give the glory to Christ. Before you received Christ you never rose above glorying in lesser things. You were proud of your church, or of your family. Of your connections with this or that person. But something has happened now. Christ has come in. With Thomas you stand there, you bow in spirit and you say to Christ, "My Lord and my God!"

"The earnest of our inheritance"
Ephesians 1:14

The word "earnest" is used only by Paul in the New Testament. It probably had its origin from the Phoenician traders. A transaction would be made, and one party would hand over to the other "earnest money," a part payment. It established the deal. It was an instalment. But it was more than an instalment, it was a pledge and guarantee that the remainder would, in due course, be honoured and paid over.

Paul reminds us that, as Christian believers, we have received the "earnest of our inheritance," the instalment and the pledge of our final salvation. "You heard the word of truth, the gospel of our salvation," says the apostle. "You trusted in Christ for salvation, and you were sealed with that Holy Spirit of promise." This earnest, then, is the new life, eternal life, which Christ gives to all who truly believe in him: it is the indwelling Spirit of the risen Saviour.

Will you notice three simple, yet wonderful things about this earnest of our salvation?

(1) It is an instalment of the *same kind* as the full and final inheritance. The believer in Christ possesses life of the *same kind* as the life to be. The spiritual life of the true Christian is the same in kind as the glorified life hereafter, the same in *kind* though not in degree or glory. The new life is at peace with God; the new life has the new look—it looks on fellowmen differently; it is no longer enmeshed and entangled in the vain rivalries, the pride and vain glory of this world. It has an open window looking out on eternal things; it has a new scale of

values; it views things, judges things, from a new vantage ground in Christ; it seeks God's glory in all things. It is indeed an instalment of the believer's full inheritance. We Christians too seldom and too little display this real instalment. The disparity, the discrepancy is not a challenge to the truth of God's Word, it's a challenge to *us* who profess and call ourselves *Christians*. We are apt to believe with our heads so much about the Cross and the Resurrection, and to appropriate and experience so little in our hearts.

(2) But while the earnest instalment is the same in kind, this is only an *instalment*. The same in kind but only a tiny fraction in degree of the full and final inheritance. It has not, as yet, entered into man's heart what good things God has prepared for them that love him. Behold what manner of love the Father has bestowed on us here and now, calling us "sons of God." But wait! "It does not yet appear what we shall be."

(3) There is one other thing about the earnest of our inheritance. This "*earnest*" implies not only present privilege and guarantee; it also implies *obligation*. We are in danger of forgetting this. In accepting the earnest-money, you knowingly and solemnly place yourself under an obligation to go through with the transaction. You have believed on Christ? You have received the earnest? You have been baptised into Christ? Then you are his by all the ties and bonds of redeeming love. You are not your own, you are bought with a price; you are sealed with the Holy Spirit of promise. You cannot, you simply *cannot* go back to the world. To do so is to insult the Spirit of grace and to trample underfoot the Son of God.

The gospel brings unspeakable privileges and "untellable" prospects of glory. But may God the Holy Spirit, remind us that it also brings solemn responsibilities and obligations.

Loving His Appearing

God's saints, his saved ones, are not in darkness as the unbelieving world is, but they are children of the light. "You are not in darkness that that day should overtake you as a thief" (1 Thess. 5:4). They have a right and a spiritual ability to read the signs of the times in which they are living. Hence Jesus urges his followers to "look at the fig trees and all the trees. When you see them putting forth their buds you know that summer is near. When you see these things coming to pass then you know that the day is near" (Luke 21:29–31).

These signs of the times are of three kinds. First, there are signs in the *organised church*, that is the church made up of all the different local gatherings, assemblies and congregations throughout the world. Second, there are signs in the *world*, outside the professing church. Third, as we considered in the previous chapter,[1] there are scriptures for signs among the *Jews*.

We have said enough to show how momentous is the teaching of the New Testament regarding the signs of the second coming among the Jews. We looked especially at Luke 21:24, and at Romans 11. It appears evident that we are on the eve of something very like what Paul anticipates in Romans. But to try to pretend that false teaching and apostasy have not come in, that out in the world people are not living for themselves to an exceeding degree, is just foolish, and not facing the facts.

We will consider the practical and spiritual lessons of the second coming. We will do this by seeing what the New

---

[1] Chapter Five of *The Appearing of Jesus* (Ian Shaw, 2014).

Testament writers say about the other two kinds of signs, those in the organised church, and those out in the world.

Signs in the Church

Our interest in the signs of the second coming of Christ should spring from our desire to know the mind of Christ, so that we might come nearer to him and serve him better. If we know what to expect we will not be dismayed and confounded when we see things happening around us, whether in the church or the world. God's word has told us very clearly that in the professing church the day of Christ will not come except there come first a falling away. The actual word is apostacy. That apostacy will be in the professing church because there cannot be a falling away in the world. People who are not Christians have nothing to fall *from*. In the same way some people talk about revival as something that must come to the world. But you cannot revive what has never had life. The revivals which God is from time to time pleased to send begin with God's own people, who have grown cold, careless, worldly and indifferent. Falling away applies to a professing church, to Christendom, and to a people that call themselves Christian and have made a profession of Christianity.

We read of this apostacy especially in 2 Thessalonians 2:3, "The day will not come except there comes a falling away first." In the great prophetic 24th chapter of Matthew the Lord Jesus says, "The love of many will wax cold" (Matt. 24:12). This will happen in the church because the love of the *world* for Jesus could not wax cold, for it was never warm. They never had any love for Jesus. That is a sign in the professing church. In the last days there will be a *form* of godliness in the church, which keeps Christian observance going but denies the power (2 Tim.

3:5). The life and vitality has gone. There is the form of worship—the sacraments and religion—but it is the framework without the real content.

Together these things constitute apostacy. These things are happening now on a very big scale around us. Love is waxing cold, and there is a falling away. A man was talking to me very recently about a relative whom he had just met. He said, "You know that lady, she used to go to this church. But you must not so much as mention these things to her now. She will almost walk out on you. She has prospered in the world, married well, and has quite a lot of money. The world seems to her to give her all she needs. She has no room or time for Jesus." Whether such people are saved eternally it is not for us to judge, but it illustrates this sign of the times, that the world is getting a hold on God's professing people. Satan always has exploited the world, but it is happening now as never before. One of the saddest things in a faithful minister's experience is to experience the love of many waxing cold.

Satan does not often entice us directly to apostacy, almost as if God does not allow him to do so. Rather, he uses bait, like a fisherman. His favourite bait to catch Christians is the world. He dangles the world before our eyes. He does it with different people in quite different ways, but it is the same basic ploy. He is very clever and subtle, using this present world to cool off our love for Christ, rob our time and energy, and sap our thoughts. We lose that first glow and appetite for spiritual things, and that new-born grace when we long to know more about the Lord Jesus Christ. I think it is fair to say that this is happening because the world has never before been such a wonderfully fascinating, alluring place as it is at the present time, with all its inventions, technology, human amenities, and facilities for travel and broadening one's horizons. This is not a sin in itself, but Satan exploits it, and says,

> Ah, give your whole thought to this as an end in itself. Leave him out, the word out, and the means of grace. After all, you cannot see these things. They are all *unseen*. I am offering you things that can be *seen*. Fall down and worship me and I will give you the kingdoms of the world.

Satan takes this approach continually with the people of God, and more so as he knows his time is short (Rev. 12:12). There is a mystery in this knowledge of Satan which we do not understand. You may hear people laugh at the idea of Satan thinking like this, but we cannot express it any other way. We have to put it into language in the same way we have to put the mind of God into language. They are personalities. We talk of God as if he were a man, and we talk of Satan as if he were a man. But Satan whispers urgently, "You go on laughing at these people who preach and teach. They are talking about God as though he has got arms, legs and eyes! Ha! Ha! Very funny!"

People who think in this way usually want us to let go of the truth because we use these anthropomorphisms thinking of the deity in the form of a man. Yet we have reason for thinking of him in the form of a man, because we know Jesus, who is the Son of God incarnate, and God understands the limitations of our language. There is a real truth under the language that we use, and we cannot let it go. We will not be frightened, intimidated and ridiculed out of it. We know that this is truth, and we will be on our guard lest Satan should cause our love to wax cold.

There is also the rejection of what the bible calls sound, whole, healthy, full doctrine and teaching. "They will not en dure sound doctrine" (2 Tim. 4:3). "In the last days know this that some will depart from the truth" (1 Tim 4:1). Peter warned that in the last days some will bring in destructive, soul-damaging teaching (2 Peter 2:1). Such teaching is very plausible and has a flavour of Christianity about it, otherwise we would not be troubled by it. But it leaves out the saving doctrines, the essential truths. One of Satan's emphases, now rather old, was on the word "Modernism." The assumption behind this word was that you could not be up to date unless you questioned the historical accuracy of many parts of the Bible. More recently one of his traps has been to intimidate Christians by the word "fundamental." Satan has coined out of it the word "Fundamentalist." If anyone calls you a Fundamentalist you are supposed to shrink, shrivel and apologise! If you are a Fundamentalist you will be laughed at. I agree that Satan has captured a little truth in it. He always makes sure of that. There are some wooden-headed Christians who have been cranky about their exposition of some of these precious doctrines, and have given cause for ridicule. So Satan frightens others by that. At its best, however, to be a Fundamentalist means you believe what God's word says. You believe the great, fundamental doctrines of the Christian faith without any apology or vaporising them away.

Jesus said, unless you return to your first love and repent I will come and remove the lampstand out of its place (Rev 2:5), and some local lampstands in our cities and villages have been removed out of their places. God has not promised to perpetuate lampstands! He has promised that the gates of hell will not prevail against his true church (Matt. 16:18), but he has not made any promise about a particular local church. If the ministry, teaching or people of a congregation fall away, God will come and judge it. There are people in the world who want life, but we are living in days when many churches are dead.

Signs in the World

The second coming of Christ, Jesus reminds us, will be just as it was in the days of Noah. They were marrying, eating, drinking, and carrying on with the ordinary things of life, as though nothing mattered. Then the flood came and destroyed them all. It was like that also in the days of Lot. They were marrying, eating, drinking, building, planting, buying and selling, and then God rained fire and brimstone from heaven on Sodom and the cities of the plain, and they were all destroyed. It will be like that, Jesus says, before I, the Son of Man, am revealed, when the veil is drawn back and you see me as I really am (Luke 17:26–30). In other words, this sign that Jesus mentioned is one of utter indifference, of smugness and "couldn't-care-less-ness."

It always has been like that, but it is increasingly so. A pretence of caring has disappeared. People give themselves up to their business, garden or holiday, and they have a very plausible excuse why they should do so. But they are living for this life and this world, as in the days of Noah and Lot before those judgements, and also as in the last days, before the judgement of God descends for a last time on an unbelieving world.

Many who quote Jesus and take his words for their texts, leave all this out, not enduring sound doctrine. They cannot stand the parts of this teaching which do not fit in with human philosophies and reason. The choice is stark. We *either* have to say that these interpretations are wrong because they are sin-marred, and the bible is right, because it is God-given and God-breathed; *or* we must conclude that the bible is all moonshine, and we will just give up the whole business and hope for the best. Those who are wise unto salvation are going to cling to God's word because it has a way of being invariably right.

There are other signs in the world mentioned in the epistles. One is *fear*. The world does not carry its fear on its sleeve. It does not always let you see, but sometimes you *do* see. For example, you may hear in the media of suicides of prominent people. Going behind the scenes you find, although that man or woman had everything the world could give, there was a fear lurking in their minds and hearts. Jesus said that in the last days men's hearts will fail them for fear of those things that are coming (Luke 21:26).

In the days when the nuclear threat was in the front line of news one could repeatedly discern that worldly fear. For the time being that seems to be in abeyance. But there remains a fear of those things that are coming to pass on the earth. Sometimes leading politicians, because they know more than we know, have expressed this inherent fear.

Another sign the scripture speaks of is *peace*. Everyone wishes for peace. Those who are Christians and children of light know that peace can only come in God's way, but the world wants peace and does not care how it comes. Such peace is often a false peace, and God's word says, "When they shall cry peace and safety then sudden destruction cometh as travail upon a woman with child" (1 Thess. 5:3). A lasting peace cannot come through people in high places who are without God. Do you think peace could be made with Nebuchadnezzar, even if he were to go round the country with a smile on his face?

We do not need to be afraid. We are God's children, but we need to be intelligent children of God, and to cling to God's word when it has thrown so much light on the false ways on the world. We cannot trust *anything* in the world. We can only trust God's word and God's Christ. When you and I reach this understanding we have made a good distance spiritually. We will then see through the things of time and sense, and yet go on using them in the right way, without any panic but looking to Jesus with our hand in his, fearless of what will come to pass.

A further sign is that in the last days people will be lovers of *pleasure* more than lovers of God. That word pleasure does not just mean fairgrounds, or going to a concert. Those things are only secondary. But the central thought is how can I please *myself*, and not how can I please God. It is a life that is revolving round myself, everlastingly turning everything to the big 'I' as centre. It revolves round me for my comfort, prosperity, glory, benefit and pleasure. A life lived in this way is in no sense of the word sacrificed to God and Jesus. Whoever saves his life shall perish and lose it, but they who lose their life for Jesus' sake and the gospel's, they, and only they, will save it.

This fear of things to come, and search for peace and pleasure, returns our thoughts to the spirit of antichrist. It is interesting that recent studies of the use of Greek prefixes, especially from archaeological discovery, have shown that 'anti' does not mean so much "against" as "false" or "pseudo." That is very illuminating. It is not that people do not want a Christ. They do want somebody, and they do want religion. That is in their blood and bones. But they do not want *this* Christ, who sheds his blood for sinners. The central meaning of the false, pseudo-Christ is that the final man of sin will meet this longing of the human heart out in the world. They want a man to unify them. There is a craving out in Christendom for *union*. Church leaders say, "Let's all come together, whether we are Roman

Catholic, Buddhist, Moslem, Baptist or Methodist. We must find the best in us all, and drop those things that are repugnant to this and that person." The antichrist will be the person ready on the scene to take the reins.

You may perhaps accuse me of being a pessimist. Not at all! No-one is a pessimist who belongs to Christ. I aim simply to be true to what God's word says, and I am not going to yield on that point to any humanism, or any humanist (so-called) gospel, because it will never work. The bible does not lead us up the garden path, but it deals with realities and stark facts.

Unity is quite different from union. You need not let go your sacred, solemn principles to have unity. Christians who meet in unity have not come together and said, "Well, I'm no longer going to believe such and such a thing." They all love the Lord Jesus, and believe they are redeemed only by his precious blood. They believe that he died in the sinner's place, rose bodily from the grave, and is coming again in person. They have unity and fellowship. This is unity, not uniformity or union, and unity is possible wherever God's people are together.

Loving His Appearing

In the light of all these signs, what kind of men, women and young people ought we to be? God's word is very clear. We should be people who love his appearing (2 Tim. 4:8). You and I dare to say we love Jesus, but we do not seem to love his appearing! If we had a lover on the human plane, and that lover was away from us, would we say that we loved him or her, but show no desire for them to come? If so, no-one would believe us! You could talk eloquently about the person you claim to love but no-one would believe you. You would be crazy about him or her, crazy with desire. Do we really love Jesus or do we love this present world? There are four ways in which we will show that we love his appearing.

First, saints are to *look for* his appearing. "We look for the Saviour" (Phil. 3:20), and "for that blessed hope and the glorious appearing of the great God and our Saviour Jesus Christ" (Titus 2:13). That is the outlook of a Christian. What are you looking for? What are the folk in the world looking for? They are looking for a pay rise, and for the enjoyment of a holiday, of retirement and a pension. But what about illness and death, and all the things that must and will happen in this fleeting world? Such people have nothing to look for. They are living in a world that is roofed in, and are looking at a ceiling, without any hope and no windows. But the child of God should be looking for that blessed hope, and not looking for death, which has come into the world because of sin. Death for Christians is only a gateway. They are looking for the coming of Jesus. The bride is looking for her bridegroom.

Second, we are to *wait* for him. We are "waiting for the coming" (1 Cor. 1.7), and in 1 Thessalonians, the loveliest epistle on the second coming, Paul says we are waiting for his son from heaven (1 Thess. 1:10). "Waiting" means we can take it, and stick it out, because we have something to look and wait for. We can put up with the misunderstanding, hardship, and persecution. We can endure not having some of the things the world calls good, and thinks we are silly not to enjoy. We can put up with it, because we are waiting patiently, getting on with the work and service of the Kingdom, which may seem so hard, lonely, and fruitless.

Third, we have to be *ready* (Matt. 24:44). However clear the signs in the church and the world, the coming of the Son of Man will be unexpected. The door closed against the virgins who were not ready is sad if not painful in its complete finality (Matt. 25:10).

There is a phrase I never fully understand, in Peter, where we are urged to be "looking for and hasting unto the coming of the day of God' (2 Peter 3:12). I remember in my very raw days, in one of my first efforts at speaking I had the impertinence to talk about hastening the coming of Christ. When you are very young, you talk about things you don't know anything about! I told these brethren they should hasten the day of the Lord's coming, and rather ungraciously a man got up and said "Our brother's quite wrong. You can't hasten the day of the Lord's coming. It's fixed. The Lord knows when he's coming, and nothing you can do can hasten it." But he didn't go on to tell me what it *did* mean! He just squashed me! Perhaps he did me good!

We are to look, wait and be ready for his coming. But the bible ends on perhaps the most wonderful thought of all. We are to *pray* and *long* for it. "Amen, even so come Lord Jesus" (Rev. 22:20). I wonder how many readers can pray these words at the close of this short book. Does your heart say, "Amen, Come Lord Jesus"? A complete change has taken place between the beginning and the end of the bible. The *beginning* records the entry of sin, death and judgement. The *last* thought of the bible is of a people who have been redeemed, their entire outlook changed, and their whole heart set upon things above, so they can pray "Come Lord Jesus." Where is our heart? It is where our treasure is. Who or what is our treasure? Is it in this world? If so, like Babylon, our treasure is collapsing, and people will stand and say of us, "Alas! Alas! That great city! For in one hour so great riches is come to nought!" (Rev. 18:16–19).

Come, Lord Jesus!

The Life of the Church

In the previous section we have seen how Leslie Land took the whole of the bible seriously in his messages about the Christian life. In this section we find the same underlying commitment, this time applied to how the Christian should understand the way God's word applies to the life of the church.

The nature and spiritual expectations of church membership are addressed in the opening piece on "Joining the Church." His heartfelt concern for Christian unity can detected on many occasions, but it was dealt with openly and fully in his message on "The Unity of the Spirit" given late in 1952. This can be read alongside his powerful message on revival that had been delivered in 1950. In Chapter Three we saw his observation as early as January 1948 that "Already God has been pleased to grant us signs of a spiritual revival, which has gladdened all our hearts."

He felt the need to speak about the Lord's Supper more than once during his time in Leicester. The example included here— "What Do You Mean by this Service?"—was preached in the year following his commencement in Leicester. It is especially helpful in the form it takes, imagining the answers parents might give to a child who asks.

Joining the Church

"I want to join the church," says one. "I see no point in joining the church," says another. "Perhaps you ought to say something on what it means to join the church," may be your own response.

The "Church"

The term "church" in the New Testament is used in at least two different ways. Sometimes it is used to describe that great, innumerable company of men and women of every time, nation and language who have been redeemed by the precious blood of the Lord Jesus Christ. In other words, the term "church," in its general sense, applies to the great fellowship of true believers. Using the word in this sense, for example, Jesus said, "On this rock I will build my church" (Matt. 16:18). The apostle Paul, writing to the Ephesians, said God "gave him as head over all things to the church, which is his body" (Eph. 1:22–23).

Sometimes, however, the word "church" is used in the New Testament in a geographical, local sense. For example, "the church of God at Corinth," "the church which is in his house," or "the church of the Laodiceans." When used in this way the word "church" refers to a restricted number of Christian believers dwelling and worshipping together in a particular locality. It may refer to a single congregation ("in his house") or perhaps to a number of congregations in a city or region (e.g., "great fear came upon the whole church," or "the church throughout all Judea and Galilee and Samaria").

Nowadays, of course, we use the word "church" in other senses too. In parts of the world, for example, people sometimes speak of "church" as distinct from "chapel." Or we may speak of the church as a building: "I met her at church." The New Testament does not use the word church in these senses.

The Church as the Body of Christ

We saw above that in the New Testament the church is spoken of as the body of Christ. Indeed, this is the only kind of body which Jesus has now in the world. He came to earth in a body at his first advent in order to die on Calvary as an atonement for our sins. On Easter morning he arose from the dead with a glorified, incorruptible body, and forty days later he ascended to heaven, bodily from the Mount of Olives, with the promise that "This Jesus, who was taken up from you into heaven, will come in the same way as you saw him go into heaven" (Acts 1:11).

Until then—throughout all the time between his first and second advents—Jesus looks upon his true church as his body in the world. Christ is the head of this spiritual body, and all true believers throughout the world are spoken of as "the body of Christ and individually members of it" (1 Cor. 12:27).

We see then that in Scripture the church of Jesus Christ is not a denomination or a sect or movement. It is a fellowship of saved men and women, girls, and boys. All who are trusting the Lord Jesus as their personal Saviour and are "born again" through the Holy Spirit constitute the church of Jesus Christ. We see therefore that, while salvation is a personal, individual matter of personal faith in Christ, the New Testament unfolds the sequel to salvation as fellowship—the fellowship of the body of Christ. A great part of this church has, of course, already gone to be with Christ. We sometimes speak of "the church militant" (here on earth) and "the church triumphant" (in heaven).

The church of Christ in the world is not, in God's eyes, not just a lot of Christians, but rather a living organism, like a body. A body is not just an aggregate of parts but a unity—a whole being, notable for its diversity rather than its uniformity. In a body we find diversity in unity. Each living part, if healthy, is controlled and governed by the head, and fulfils a vital part and function. Some parts are less physically attractive than others, in the church as well as the human body, and yet in both cases they seem to have more honour of use and function placed on them. God, says the apostle, has "tempered the body" in this way, so that there is no schism in the body. Paul explains this in 1 Corinthians 12.

The Vital Importance of the Local Church

There are many sincere Christian believers who wholeheartedly accept the bible's teaching about the body of Christ and yet hold themselves aloof, in a measure, and refuse to commit themselves to any local church. Let me express very clearly my personal conviction on this matter. It is, I believe, a sad thing and out of line with God's revealed will and purpose when truly born-again Christians refrain from joining and clearly aligning themselves with a local church.

You may say, "I am a member of the one great true church of Christ, so what else matters?" There is very much else that matters. The one great church of Christ is a reality from God's point of view and is well known to him as he looks down upon this world. But from our limited human point of view, we must admit that this universal church of Christ never meets together—cannot do so—in one place or time for worship, prayer, fellowship or anything at all. In spite of jets, comets, space travel and so on, you and I have to spend most of our time in a particular locality. The only church we know and meet in practice is the local church—the church of God in Corinth, in the town High Street, in so-and-so's property, and so on. It is particular local churches that are the church of Christ in miniature, in which we worship, pray and serve and give for the extension of Christ's kingdom in the world. It is in fellowship with this local church that we lay our hands of those who the Holy Spirit separates and sends out into the service of the King of Kings

A person who tells me that he does not belong to a local church because he belongs to the church which is Christ's body reminds me of someone who does not keep the Lord's Day because to him or her "every day is the Lord's Day." Practical experience has shown all too clearly that "every day is the Lord's Day" means no Lord's Day at all! I fear also that all too often refusal to commit oneself to the local church means no church at all.

Christians depend on one another for fellowship in worship, prayer, giving and in many other ways. There are missionaries to be cared for and supported; there are pastors, ministers, teachers, elders and deacons to be appointed. There are properties to be maintained and finances to be administered. These and a thousand other matters of spiritual import involve, and rightly so, the taking and shouldering of responsibilities by God's people. How can such God-ordained work and witness be maintained unless true believers band themselves together as we see in the New Testament?

Faithful, bible-teaching ministries and vigorously live spiritual churches do not spring up like mushrooms overnight. They are the outcome of sacrificial prayer, giving and labours of love. Such Spirit-filled centres of faithful preaching, work and witness are made possible under God by the constancy, faithfulness and reliability of God's true children in the local church, who are present, wherever possible, at the means of grace. It all takes tangible form and expression in and through the local church, the body of Christ in miniature. We are saved individually, but heaven is a *fellowship* of believers. The closing vision of the bible is not of a straggling stream of spiritual freelancers entering heaven, but of a Holy City coming down from God out of heaven.

Are you a truly born-again Christian? If so, are you doing everything in your power to support and further the witness and work of Christ in and through the church in your locality, shouldering its responsibilities as well as sharing its privileges? No true Christian should be a spectator in the local church. We live in momentous times. It is only as spiritually minded, consecrated believers are bound together in the bonds of love for Christ and the word, that a living, Christ-centred witness can be maintained.

If you love the Saviour and his word, and are jealous for his name and the spread of the gospel, then, in the Saviour's name, commit yourself unhesitatingly and unreservedly to the privileges and responsibilities of membership of a local church where Christ is exalted and his word faithfully preached.

"The unity of the Spirit ...
There is one body"
Ephesians 4:3–4

In what ways do these statements about the "unity of the Spirit" and "the one body" express a reality, a truth? How, if at all, may we reconcile God's word with denominationalism? One thing is very clear from the Scriptures; there is one God, one Christ, one cross, one Holy Spirit, and therefore there can only be one church. We hear Christians speak of *two* churches, one visible and the other invisible. Whether the church is visible or invisible depends entirely on our ability or inability to view it. God is able to view the one true church. His sight is keen, clear and accurate. Our judgement is limited and erring. We pass human judgement as to who is in the church and who is not. We cannot be sure, but he knows.

There is only one church. To you and to me it is mostly invisible. We only see a tiny part of it, and even of that tiny part (the local church) we cannot be sure; but he knows. His eye is all-searching; his judgement is unerring. God's one church is the corporate body of regenerate, born-again, believing men and women, boys and girls. They have been redeemed out of every kindred, tribe and tongue. They belong to Jesus Christ. They are the body of Christ. Its members, the corporate body, are indwelt by the Holy Spirit. It is the temple of the living God, and its unity is the unity of the Spirit.

There is widely held, and by intelligent, thoughtful Christians, another view of God's church. Those who hold this other view regard the church as a unity not only of Spirit but also of form. They speak of apostolical succession. They claim that their outward form of ministry and worship is continuous with that of New Testament times and that any other form of ministry or worship is "irregular." Now I do not believe that there is a worshipping body of people on the earth who may justly make such a claim. The Roman Catholic Church lays claim to its continuity of form more than any other body, but if you have witnessed high mass in Notre Dame Cathedral, as I have, you will readily agree that nothing could be further removed from the simplicity of form revealed in the New Testament. We noticed when talking about the Lord's Supper that one Roman Catholic writer has said that each time he celebrates the mass he seems to be looking into the upper room through the wrong end of a telescope, meaning that in the far distance there is a direct line back to that occasion. I can only agree that it must be the *wrong* end. The only apostolic succession that matters is that we should "continue steadfastly in the apostle's doctrine"; that we should love, adore and proclaim the same Saviour and be indwelt by the same Holy Spirit.

Then what of our outward forms and organisations in the church of Christ? Do they matter? We need to think clearly here. We need to remember that organisation is not of the essence or essential life of the church of Jesus Christ. Essentially, the church of Christ is an organism, not an organisation. We must not equate the church with a denomination or one particular form of its administration. It is historically true that we find organisation to be necessary to the growth and consolidation of Christian enterprise. But we must not fall for thinking that the risen Christ could not have a church in the world if there were no Baptists or Congregationalists, no Anglicans or Brethren, no Methodists or Presbyterians on the earth.

The true oneness of the church is the oneness of belonging to the body of Christ. The true and only unity of the church is the unity of the indwelling Holy Spirit. It is Christ who is the life and heart-beat of the church. Compatible with honouring Christ as the head in all things and glorifying him through the members, God has left us free to form our own organisations, and these surely will differ from time to time and from place to place.

Schism is a sin, but it is a sin against the unity of the Spirit. The sin of schism does not lie in the variety of organisations. The sin of schism lies in our denominational jealousy, self-aggrandisement and bigotry: the everlastingness of "we Baptists," "we Methodists," "we Anglicans," "we Brethren"—the "one of us" outlook, to the forgetting of the one body of Christ. That is schism, a breach of the unity of the Spirit, a sin against the Spirit of unity. As for variety of organisation among those who truly love the Lord and hold to the head in all things, such variety is only a special application at a high level of one of God's laws of his universe. By way of illustration, white light is a composite unit. Similarly, a symphony made up of a lot of repetitions of the same note would be a monotonous absurdity. True unity in anything is a composite. Anything else is a mere aggregate, like a desert of sand. No one would choose to live in a desert. Any mere letting-go of our individual denominational characteristics and principles might spell *union*, but never in and of itself *unity*. The true church of Jesus Christ has a rich diversity of gifts and characters, and a unity which is the unity of the Spirit. There is one body, but that body is no mere arithmetical sum of believers but a vast and composite organism, composed of redeemed men and women.

When I meet a Christian, who says he or she belong to no denomination, I just wonder if it means that they hold no clear convictions. Personally, I am a Baptist and a Baptist by conviction. Not simply because my parents were Baptists, or just because of earlier associations with that denomination. However, I find it difficult to enjoy fellowship with others simply on the ground of their saying they are Baptists. If they do not give the living Christ the first place, if they do not stand by the authority of the Holy Scriptures in the plain, honest-to-goodness accepted evangelical sense of that statement, then in all sincerity I confess that I find it impossible to experience real fellowship with them, since for me the unity of the Spirit has been destroyed. The real secret of spiritual unity lies not in organisation but in a vital relationship to the living Christ, by the Holy Spirit, through the word of God.

Let me say here that I experience a peculiar joy in ministering to a fellowship which is truly inter-denominational in character. I stress *inter*-denominational as distinct from *un*denominational. There is the unity the Spirit in that the crucified, ascended and returning, personal Christ is altogether central and holds the fellowship together, rather than any common form. Moreover, I experience a richness of fellowship in serving on the Home Council of an inter-denominational missionary society. Having said all that, I am still a Baptist, unashamed and uncompromising, though I lay no claim to being what some keen denominationalists appear to call "a good Baptist." Indeed, I sometimes think that "good Baptists" are perhaps the biggest hindrance to "Baptist Advance." I am jealous that every Baptist colleague who visits this pulpit should confront the people, not with an organisation, but with the living Christ, and that he should always preach and teach the "things concerning him in all the Scripture."

Let us avoid schism like the plague. But let us go all out, faithful and loyal to our particular inheritance and convictions, to advance the kingdom of God by winning souls for Christ. It is more of Christ we need today, the living Christ. If we are to keep the unity of Spirit in the bond of peace, we must each and all draw nearer to Christ. There is one body. It is the body of Christ!

"What do you mean by this service?"
Exodus 12:26–27

"What do you mean by this service?" So the Hebrew child asked its parents concerning that ancient feast in Israel, the Lord's Passover. "Christ our Passover is sacrificed for us," says Paul. Why shouldn't our children watch us keep the Lord's supper? On the way home they have a right to ask us, "What does this service mean?" We must be ready to give them a plain, simple, truthful answer. From time to time we need to reconsider the sacraments of the church in the light of God's word, for it is all too easy to *add to* or to *take from* the real meaning of these ordinances; to say "Wouldn't it be nice if we did so-and-so," without any reference to God's word. After all, they are *God's* ordinances; *he* designed them; *he* gave them through Christ to the church. They concern the Lord Jesus Christ.

A Historic Faith

"What do you mean by this service?" Well, firstly, we will tell our children something that will interest them. "Is it true? Did it really happen?", they may ask. We will tell them that the simple feast has been kept by those who love the Lord Jesus, all down the centuries. Like a golden chain of remembrance, it links us with the upper furnished room in Jerusalem on Calvary's eve. Yes, our faith is an *historic* faith. A Roman Catholic writer has said that when he attends the mass, he seems to be looking through the wrong end of a telescope right back into the "upper room." I have watched the mass in Notre Dame

Cathedral, Paris, but I fear its elaborate ceremonial reminded me of anything but the "upper room." We can truthfully say of this simple table that it links us with that "last" yet "first" supper of 2,000 years ago. But remember, the supper was spread on the Passover table. The Passover meal was over when Jesus took the bread and the cup of blessing into his hands. The golden chain links to another chain, for God's people had been keeping the Passover feast all down the centuries, away back to that Passover night when the children of Israel had eaten their last supper in Egypt in haste, a piece of Passover lamb in one hand, maybe, and a staff in the other. Yes, all down the ages, people have been celebrating the fact that God has set his heart on redeeming us, for the Passover Lamb looked forward, just as the bread and wine look backward to the Lamb of God who bears away the sin of the world.

A Harder Thing

"What do you mean by this service?" We must tell our children a harder thing. Every detail of this simple supper speaks of *death*. Tell them the bread is *broken*, tell them the wine is *outpoured*. Tell them the wine is separated from the bread. And the words fit the actions. Did Jesus say "This is my body, which *lives* for you?" No! "Which is *given for you*?" Was it "this cup is my blood, which flows in the limbs which work for you?" No! 'Which is being *shed* for you?" The symbols used, the words spoken, the occasion, Passover night, everything emphasises the fact that this supper centres in the saving, atoning death of Jesus Christ on the cross. Our children may well wonder how we can be glad at such a feast but tell them that we owe everything to the fact that Jesus laid down his life for us.

He died that we might be forgiven,
He died to make us good;
That we might go at last to heaven,
Saved by his precious blood.[1]

Tell them, too, that Jesus *lives*, we do not gather round a crucifix, Jesus is *risen* from the dead. He is present at the feast. He does not come to us through the elements in any physical or mechanical way, like water through a pipe. He is not in the bread, he is not in the wine, for they speak of death, and our Saviour *lives*.

If you own a house, show them the trust deeds. When these deeds become mine, the house is mine. The house is not in the deeds, but give me the deeds and the house is mine. Jesus said, "Do this in remembrance of me," and every time I "do this," I know in a special way, and I am sure that Jesus is mine.

A Covenant

"What do you mean by this service?" Tell them it means that God has made a covenant, a *new* covenant with us. A covenant is an agreement between two parties, in this case God and sinners, and a lavishly one-sided agreement where God gives and we take, "Take and eat this." We will read Jeremiah to our children. "Behold, the days are coming," God says, "when I will make a *new* covenant with the house of Israel ... not like the covenant that I made with their fathers on the day when I took them by the hand to bring them out of the land of Egypt, my covenant that they broke ... *this* is the covenant that I will make with the house of Israel ... I will put my law within them, and I will write it on their hearts" (Jer. 31:31–33). In its

---

[1] Cecil F. Alexander (1818–1895), "There is a green hill."

simplest terms, God has made it possible for sinful men and women, boys and girls to have their hearts cleansed and changed, so that their lives and characters may become really pleasing in God's holy sight, and God has done all this in and through the Lord Jesus. His blood shed on Calvary, seals and ratifies the agreement and makes it work in our lives. Every time we gather round the Lord's table, we celebrate this precious new agreement which has brought God's pardon and a new heart to all his people. Every time we keep the feast it seems to bind us a little more closely to him "who loved me and gave himself for me."

"What do you mean by this service?" Tell them it is preaching in action. "For as often as you eat this bread and drink the cup, you *proclaim* the Lord's death." Tell them it is a *prophecy*. The Jew at his Passover feast says, "Next time, in Jerusalem." The believer at the Lord's table may say, "Next time, maybe, at his coming." Even so, come, Lord Jesus!

Revival:
The Wind in the Treetops
2 Samuel 5:22–25

David had been crowned king over God's people Israel, but the Philistines, the enemies of God and his people, were ever rearing their heads. David, as a shepherd boy, had learned not to oppose them in his own strength. "You come to me with a sword and with a spear and with a javelin," he had once said to the Philistine giant, "but I come to you in the name of the Lord of hosts" (1 Sam. 17:45). Now, on the throne of Israel and again threatened by this subtle enemy, David has the good sense and faith to inquire of the Lord, "Shall I go up against the Philistines?" David, of course, might have reasoned within himself, "These Philistines are opposed to God's kingdom, the obvious and practical thing to do is to organise an attack, God is bound to follow, bound to bless my enterprise." No! David must follow the Lord, not the Lord follow David. "David inquired of the Lord." And God said to David, "You shall not go up; go around to their rear, and come against them opposite the balsam trees. And when you hear the sound of a going in the tops of the balsam trees, then rouse yourself, for then the Lord has gone out before you to strike down the army of the Philistines" (2 Sam. 5:22–25).[1] And David obeyed the Lord, and the Lord, through David, routed the Philistines.

---

[1] Land was using the King James Version. All modern translations translate "a going" as "marching.' I have followed the ESV but have retained 'going' with the sense traditionally given of the sound of a wind, because the sermon is based on the application of the sense of 'wind' for the work of the Holy Spirit.

The Philistines are out in full force against the kingdom of God today. "For we do not wrestle against flesh and blood, but against the rulers, against the authorities, against the cosmic powers over this present darkness, against the spiritual forces of evil in the heavenly places" (Eph. 6:12). Throughout our[2] Baptist denomination in Great Britain and Ireland the call has sounded to advance. Delegates to those great Assembly Meetings in London early in May must have returned to their homes and churches with a fresh glow of hope and inspiration in their hearts.[3] But how is the challenge to be met? How is the hope to be realised? We all know that enthusiasm and sincerity are in themselves utterly inadequate to the task. What we all need, what the church of God needs desperately at this time is power—power from on high. We are not lacking in organisation, in efficient machinery, in scholarship. But revival does not come that way, God may and does use these things in his service, but that for which we are looking and longing does not come that way. Revival is a movement of the Spirit of God operating in and through a people ready and prepared to receive him. The message of Whitsuntide is that the great day of the Spirit has come. Following the cross and resurrection of our Lord, power from on high has been lavishly unleashed. This power is the person of the Holy Spirit. "He dwells with you and will be in you' (John 14:17) was the promise of Jesus. The power is available, but largely unappropriated. The chief

---

[2] Land typically aligned himself with the Baptist denomination, although he was well aware of the theological frailties at its heart. For an interesting account of the history of Baptist conservative evangelicalism from the 1930s through to 1972 see Philip Hill, *The Baptist Revival Fellowship* (London: Apostolos Publishing Ltd., 2017). Melbourne Hall was to distance itself from the Baptist Union during the 1960s under his successor, Eric Gurr.

[3] E.A. Payne took over as General Secretary of the Baptist Union from 1951 and led the denomination in a strongly ecumenical direction. See Hill, *The Baptist Revival Fellowship*, chapters 2 and 3.

hindrance to revival is our unreadiness and unwillingness as Christians to wait upon God, to let God the Holy Spirit control and direct our lives. You cannot organise a revival. This sound of a going in the tops of the trees is nothing less than a movement of the Spirit of God. The command "You shall not go up" is a lesson to David, to you and to me, not to lean upon the arm of flesh, not to trust in our own resources.

"And when you hear the sound of a going in the tops of the balsam trees, then rouse yourself." This wind in the treetops is a symbol of the movement of the Spirit of God. "The wind blows where it wishes, and you hear its sound, but you do not know where it comes from or where it goes. So it is with everyone who is born of the Spirit" (John 3:7). Who hears? Those who wait upon God.

Revivals in history have always come that way. It was a mere handful of ordinary people of whom it was said, "These men have turned the world upside down." Turned the world upside down? Yes! How did they do it? Not by clever organisation, not by lots of conferences and conventions, not by rushing about here and there in their own strength. It was "while staying with them he (the risen Christ) ordered them not to depart from Jerusalem, but to wait for the promise of the Father, which, he said, 'you heard from me … you will receive power when the Holy Spirit has come upon you'" (Acts 1:4, 8). "When the day of Pentecost arrived, they were all together in one place. And suddenly there came from heaven a sound like a mighty rushing wind, and it filled the entire house where they were sitting. And divided tongues as of fire appeared to them and rested on each one of them. And they were all filled with the Holy Spirit" (Acts 2:1–4).

This indeed was the wind in the treetops for which they had waited upon God, the sign and call from heaven to rouse themselves to advance against all the Philistines of this world's darkness. It was more than the sign and the call to advance; it was the power from on high to do it. "For then the Lord has gone out before you to strike down the army of the Philistines," said God to David. The same Lord said to his disciples, "you will receive power when the Holy Spirit has come upon you, and you will be my witnesses in Jerusalem and in all Judea and Samaria, and to the end of the earth" (Acts 1:8).

It is this waiting in the "upper room" which we today find so hard, both as individual Christians, and as the church of Christ. It is so much easier to organise than to agonise. We will do anything rather than pray. Yet the most tremendous, and perhaps the most mysterious fact in all this mysterious universe is that this waiting upon God in prayer sets all the power and resources of heaven operating upon earth. "Your will be done on earth as it is in heaven" (Matt. 6:10), is not a fatalistic decree but a prayer for believers. The plain truth is we just do not like praying; we find it hard and uninteresting. We want to get down to breakfast, to the radio, to the business, to anything, but to our knees. As churches we will come together for anything rather than for prayer and waiting upon God. The result is that in many of our churches conversions have ceased—the very thing, mark you, for which we exist as churches in the world, the glory of God and the salvation of mankind. A city business concern which so miserably failed to fulfil its purpose would be driven by a sheer sense of shame either to reform itself or to close down. As churches of God we ought indeed to blush with confusion of face at this time in view of our comparative ineffectiveness against the Philistines of darkness, lawlessness and unbelief. There is no defeatism in my mind and heart. If I did not believe in the unchanging Christ, believe that his mighty power to save people and pull down Satan's strongholds is the same today as in apostolic times, I would quit the ministry right away. Christ is unchanged and un-changing; the gospel is explosive stuff; the Holy Spirit is a real person, a personal reality. But it is a law of the universe that the choicest and best gifts are never received lightly or easily. In a day of "easy believism," "slick evangelism" and "conversion-without-tears," it is still true that the deep and mighty blessings of the life eternal come by way of waiting upon almighty God, by the New Testament way of agonising in persistent prayer.

Perhaps we are too self-satisfied, too clever, too worldly-wise, too "logically-minded" to pray. Dear friends, the wonders of God in the realm of the Spirit are altogether beyond our na-tive wisdom and our petty logic. His ways are past finding out. If only we would begin today to wait upon him, to inquire of the Lord, to open the windows of our soul continually to Christ, blessing and peace and power would flow in us and through us like a river from the throne of God. When the church of Jesus Christ forsakes her false riches and self-satis-faction and in utter helplessness waits upon God, we shall hear more than the sound of a going in the treetops. The Lord him-self will go out before us, conquering and to conquer, for the great day of the Spirit will have come.

Defending the Gospel

The enduring challenge of the "Hegemony" message, given in December 1961, and that opens this final section, has been referred to several times in the account of his ministry. But he was concerned to defend the gospel throughout his time in Leicester. In August 1948 he printed his message on "The Folly of What We Preach."

A further leading theme was on the various ways God calls people into his service. The message "Are You Called?" was given in 1960, and the articles and messages he gave on the missionary call and its relationship to the local church were addressed in 1955 and again in 1960. We might equally have included this in the selection of contributions on "The Life of the Church," but Land never was a man to compartmentalise the application of his teaching and preaching. We have seen in the account of his life that the questions raised by his understanding of this issue anticipated the much greater awareness of the believers in the reformed churches a decade later.

We might have extended this final section to reflect how his science background at university and in his teaching career was manifested in a continuing curiosity of how this related to his Christian faith. He remarked on one occasion that,

> Men and women are doing wonderful things in the realm of science and technology but remember that they are lost souls. Whatever is produced at the scientific and intellectual centres of the world has the potential to destroy. The innovations of science and technology could be a blessing in a new heaven and a new earth, with all

these wonders of God's universe harnessed to Christ and to his purpose and kingdom. But do not let Satan deceive you about the prospects of a world that is without Christ. If we keep to what the scriptures say, although it sounds bleak as far as the world is concerned, we will be on the side of truth. The prospect for the world without Christ is a dark one, and an ever darkening one in scripture. For the saint, the believer in Jesus who loves his appearing, the prospect is an ever brightening one.[1]

---

[1] Land, W. Leslie, *The Appearing of Jesus* Second edition. York Publishing Services, 2014.

Hegemony
Luke 3:1-2

Christians are sometimes troubled in mind by what I would call the "arithmetic problem." We who truly love the Lord Jesus Christ and believe his word are like a drop in the ocean, compared with the rest of humanity. Think of the millions, surging to and fro daily in the great cities of the world, who never give a thought to Christ. Think of all the councils and conferences in the world where politicians, scientists, philosophers and so on meet together without even naming the name of God. This minority problem gets some people in the church down.

When we turn to the opening words of Luke chapter 3—they are very dull reading—you will find light on our problem:

> In the fifteenth year of the reign of Tiberius Caesar, Pontius Pilate being governor of Judea, and Herod being tetrarch of Galilee, and his brother Philip tetrarch of the region of Ituraea and Trachonitis, and Lysanias tetrarch of Abilene, during the high priesthood of Annas and Caiaphas, the word of God came to John the son of Zechariah in the wilderness. (Luke 3:1–2)

Here we are confronted by an impressive array of world powers and world affairs—and the word of God came to a man named John, in a desert.

"In the fifteenth year of the reign of Tiberius Caesar." The Greek word translated "reign" has come over into our English dictionaries. It is the word "hegemony." It means powerful leadership, mastery, domination. Now read Luke's dull verses again:

In the fifteenth year of the hegemony or world domination of Tiberius Caesar, Pontius Pilate being delegated to
the hegemony of Judea, and Herod, Philip and Lysanias
being vassals of this hegemony, Annas and Caiaphas being the hierarchy of the hegemony over Judaism and the
Jewish people.

If you are not awestruck and impressed you must indeed have
been to Calvary's cross and had all your values changed.

What Was the Word?

It was about God's Son. God's word is always about Jesus, his
saviour-Son. It was not about Tiberius, Pontius Pilate, Herod,
Philip or Lysanias. It was not about the religious leaders, Annas
and Caiaphas. It was about Jesus. What is more, this word of
God to John mattered more than all the words of all the Caesars
put together. It by-passed Rome, the eternal city, the city of
seven hills. It by-passed the tetrarchs and the religionists of that
day. It lighted on a man named John in a desert.

What Kind of Word?

It was a stern word. No mealy-mouthed sentiment. No plati-
tudes. It was a word about sin. God always begins there. It was
a word about judgement. Sin always leads to judgement. If God
be God, sin must be judged. It was a word about an axe being
laid to the root of the tree.

But it was also a word about deliverance and salvation. It was a
call to repent and turn to the Messiah, the Lamb of God, who
was to bear away the sin of the world.

Caesar could not bear that word. His heart was full of hegemony, the lust for power. Pontius Pilate and the tetrarchs

could not receive it either. Their hearts were under the sway and hegemony of pride and inordinate ambition. The religionists? No, they had no room for a saviour. Their hearts were dominated by the hegemony of self-righteousness. To talk to them of sin and judgement was sheer impertinence.

And so the word of God came to a man called John—in the desert.

Today

It is exactly the same in our world today. Mankind is in revolt, at enmity against God. Strange ideologies are making a desperate bid for the hegemony of mankind. God's word concerning his saviour-Son cannot be received where pride, self-love and self-righteousness hold hegemony and sway. But where there is a broken, contrite heart, a heart tired of the hegemony of self and sin, *there* the word of God will come with converting and renewing power. Where there is a desert place willing to receive him, the desert shall rejoice and blossom as the rose.

Moreover, there is a day coming when the hegemonies over this world will become the hegemony of our God and of his Christ. No arithmetic problem there! Every knee shall bow, every tongue confess that Jesus is Lord to the glory of God the father. In that day the redeemed of the Lord will shine as the sun in the kingdom of their Father.

"The folly of what we preach"
1 Corinthians 1:21

A sign of the times is the present-day attitude to preaching. We even find churches advertising services, with the promise "No Sermon"! The idea commonly held is that preaching is an intrusion upon our worship. One movement of our day, professedly Christian, cynically refers to preaching as "one man presuming to get up and give advice."[1] Even in some clearly evangelical circles "preaching" is spoken of disparagingly and the "sermon" is replaced by a "*talk*" or an "*address*."

What about this *preaching*? Let me remind you that God has *done* something in history for us men and our salvation. "God so loved that he gave..." If we say that we like *deeds* best, then the Gospel meets the challenge perfectly. God has done all that he *can* do, *needs* do, *will* do to bring sinners back again into fellowship with himself. He has done it in Jesus Christ his son, our Saviour. But Christmas is not a story in *mime*. God has clothed the drama of our salvation with words. God has spoken. He spoke in times past through the prophets; they went about *preaching*, calling people back to God, pointing them on to Christ. And when "the fullness of the time had come," we read "In those days John the Baptist came *preaching*" (Matt. 3:1). A little later we read "From that time Jesus began to *preach*" (Matt. 4:17). Then he chose and commissioned twelve disciples, saying "Go and *preach*." Still later he sent seventy others also; they went into every town and village

---

[1] I have not been able to trace the source of this quotation.

preaching (Luke 10). When Calvary and the resurrection were accomplished, we find his Spirit-filled apostles, in ever- widening circles, beginning at Jerusalem, and then in Judea, in Samaria and to the uttermost parts of the earth, *preaching, preaching, preaching*! "And every day, in the temple and from house to house, they did not cease teaching and preaching that the Christ is Jesus" (Acts 5:42).

Let us be clear, they did not go about simply "giving talks." No! One favourite New Testament word for *preaching* means to proclaim as a herald, with certainty and authority, demanding, even commanding, a hearing. *Preaching* in the New Testament has all God behind it, and this distinguishes *preaching* from all other forms of human speech. Christianity is no mysticism, no vague aesthetic feeling. It is a revelation made and given in Jesus Christ, made known by a plain, direct preached word, an "I" to a "You." All down the ages the power of God has accompanied that preached word, power to change men's lives, power "to turn the world upside down." *God* has ordained that men should *preach*. Preaching is God's idea, God's plan and method. It has pleased God by the foolishness of preaching to save those who believe. Paul asks, how shall they believe in him of whom they have not heard, and how shall they hear without a preacher, and how shall they preach except they be sent (Rom. 10:14–15)? Do you wonder that John Wesley with this magnificent New Testament conception of preaching should always preach "as a dying man to dying men"?[2] Preaching is God's gift to the church.

---

[2] He appears to be misquoting here. The words "I preached as never sure to preach again, and as a dying man to dying men" were first spoken by Richard Baxter. Words of Wesley often have been compared to Baxter. He was once asked "Mr. Wesley supposing that you know that you were to die at twelve o'clock tomorrow night, how would you spend the intervening time?" Wesley said, "Why madam, just as I intend to spend it now. I would preach this evening at Gloucester, and again at five tomorrow

It would be very interesting to trace the history of man's misuse and neglect of this gift. As the centuries rolled by, the word of God and the preaching of the word fell more and more into the background in the church's life and worship; they became buried beneath a mass of forms and ceremonies, priestly accretions and other external paraphernalia. As a result, the life of the church and its people became morally and spiritually corrupt. In the 16th Century there came a breath from heaven. We speak of the great Protestant Reformation. God took hold of men like Martin Luther, John Calvin and the Reformers, names to conjure with in Christian thought. In a word, the Reformation was a *rediscovery* of the *word of God*. It was *after* that great Reformation that many of our godly forefathers had the faith and courage to break with the fettered and state-controlled church of that day and claimed the right and the freedom to reform their life and worship by the word of God. They were labelled "Non-conformists," "Dissenters." Their children's children worship here tonight, proud in the Lord of our rich heritage, free to worship Almighty God in august and dignified simplicity, free from all the tawdry, priestly accretions of those middle ages. We need humbly to pray for our many faithful brothers and sisters in the state church at this time, who are sorely plagued and harassed by a movement in that church to lead them, if not to drive them, back again to that sorry pre-Reformation state of affairs, with its candles and crucifixes and confessionals.[3]

---

morning; after that I would ride to Tewkesbury, preach in the afternoon, and meet the societies in the evening. I would then go to Rev. Martin's house, who expects to entertain me, talk and pray with the family as usual, retire to my room at 10 o'clock, commend myself to my heavenly Father, lie down to rest, and wake up in Glory."

[3] The World Council of Churches came into existence when representatives of 147 churches met at its First Assembly in Amsterdam.

But make no mistake. Although we were labelled *Non-conformists*, *Dissenters* and Protestants—all *negative* terms—you will notice the great thing for which we stand is no *negative* thing, but something very *positive*. What is this positive thing? The Reformation brought the word of God and the preaching of the word of God back again into the centre of church life and worship. It is no accident that the pulpits in our free churches are of prominent dimensions, central and lifted up. It is the word of God that is exalted. The wearing of a simple gown has no priestly significance whatever. It is intended to serve as a simple and dignified clothing to mark the *office*, not the man— the *office* of preacher.[4]

Do not be intimidated, dear friend, if someone says, "Oh, *you* go to chapel to hear a man preach." The remark reveals a very shallow understanding. It is a caricature of a profound and lovely truth. Actually, we gather about the feet of God with an intentional simplicity, to hear the word of God as it is proclaimed and preached from a pulpit, as it is silently and symbolically proclaimed from the Lord's table and from an open watery grave. Our very prayers breathe the word of God. Our spiritual songs reiterate and re-affirm our faith in Christ. Shame on us if our preaching has been replaced by a "five-minute talk." Shame on us if our prayers have become flights of pious oratory or vain repetitions. Shame on us if our hymnology has substituted daffodils, subjective phenomena and sloppy sentimentalities for the great objective facts of our Redeemer and Lord.

But note, it is not so much the act of preaching that the apostle has in mind in this text, but rather the *thing preached*, the "folly" of the thing preached! The preaching of the cross

---

[4] Land wore a black gown when preaching.

is folly to those who are perishing, but to us who are being saved it is the power of God (1 Cor. 1:18). Some people, says Paul, want a *sign*. "We would be Christians," they say, "if only God would show his hand, and do *this* or *that*." Others, Paul says, are seeking wisdom. "We would become Christians," they say, "if only you would give us a sound philosophical, intellectual basis for our belief." But no, it hasn't pleased God to save anyone by magic or by intellectual wisdom. It *has* pleased God by the preaching of Jesus Christ and him crucified—a message which seems foolish judged by this world's standards—to save them that believe.

Are You Called?

"I feel called to full time service."

We have often heard this. How may we know that we are really called? What constitutes a call? What can we learn from the Bible about the *necessity* and the *nature* of such a call?

The Necessity of a Call

We may all agree that a call is necessary. Jesus said, "I have sent them into the world" (John 17:18). Paul wrote, "How are they to preach unless they are *sent*?" (Rom. 10:15). God *sent* his Son. Christ *sent* his apostles. There is a similarity although not an identity between these. Christ was sent to redeem. The apostles were sent to proclaim redemption.

We in turn are sent; we are under authority. We are not apostles. They wrote holy Scripture, we apply it. Their call was extraordinary, direct from Christ. They were endowed with supernatural gifts to match the need. Today we do not look for extraordinary calls of this nature—visions, oracles, etc. The Scripture revelation is complete. "This gospel of the kingdom will be preached throughout the whole world as a testimony to all nations and then the end will come" (Matt. 24:14). The course of the church is prescribed. Its ordinances are laid down. "Behold, I am with you always, to the end of the age."

Our call today, then, is of the ordinary type. We have the Word of truth, the world of need and the Holy Spirit to honour the Word. However, we should be clear—very clear—about the call.

The Nature of the Call

The call has two parts. It has inward and outward aspects.

Inward

We must be sure inwardly of a call from God, sure that we are in the will of God. How may we be sure? If we are not to expect a dream, a vision, or a light from heaven, how may we know that we are called inwardly? By two things. Ability and willingness. God calls us when he makes us able and willing.

Ability. The Spirit of God fitted or equipped people to build the tabernacle. Much more will he equip for the building of his spiritual temple under the new covenant. Presidents and prime ministers choose ambassadors that are fitted for the task. More so God gives needful gifts, graces and abilities. This is the first mark of an inward call, his enabling.

Paul speaks of God's enabling several times: "Who has made us sufficient to be ministers of the new covenant" (2 Cor. 3:6). "I thank him who has given me strength, Christ Jesus our Lord" (1 Tim. 1:12). An elder should be "able to teach" (1 Tim. 3:2). When God puts a person into his ministry he first enables. There are, of course, different degrees of abilities, but God-given abilities there should and must be.

Willingness. Ability does not constitute a call. There must be willingness. God makes us willing. There should be a strong inclination. "If anyone *aspires to* the office…" (1 Tim. 3:1). The inward call, therefore, consists in being fitted and made willing by God. It is tragic when people, neither fitted nor willing, take upon themselves the ministry of the gospel either from some personal motive or because others have over-persuaded them.

Outward

The inward call is not enough. With a view to order in the church of Christ an outward call is necessary, a call by the church of Christ on earth. In the Old Testament, God called Aaron to serve at the altar. But he also had to be anointed and purified, set apart, by the "church" (Ex. 28.3; Num. 3:3). God called Peter to go to Cornelius, but Cornelius called him too. 'Set apart for me Barnabas and Saul' said the Holy Spirit (Acts 13:2). Yes, the Holy Spirit had chosen them, made them able and willing, but he called on the church to separate them.

This raises a difficult question. By whom is this outward call to be made? History reveals three claimants to this power to give an external call:

1. Ordinary believers in the church.
2. The spiritual overseers in the church.
3. The state in some form.

In the organised church of today we meet with a confusing medley of these three. In addition, we find a great number of freelancers who claim to be called inwardly, and who repudiate any need for an outward call. What can we say about each of these claimants?

Ordinary believers. It seems clear from scripture that there should be a call from the believers in the church. 120 believers had a part in calling Matthias in the place of Judas (Acts 1.15–16, 23). Later the apostles called together "the full number of the disciples" telling them to pick out from among them 'seven men of good repute, full of the Holy Spirit and of wisdom" (Acts 6:2–3).

It seems clear in the light of scripture, that in the measure that any local church is deeply spiritually minded, filled with the Holy Spirit, and grounded in the word of God, that church should be well able to give an *outward* call to a true man of God for service at home or abroad, knowing and rightly judging them to be such a one as will make known to others the whole counsel of God.

The same surely applies to missionaries to some degree. Missionaries should have proved themselves in a local church as men and women of God, given to the word and prayer, labouring to win souls in and through the local fellowship, ready and willing, if asked to do so, to "serve tables" for a period. The church is not there just to meet the financial needs of such people, though she will do that readily and sacrificially if all else is as it should be.

The church, as ordinary believers, should send out ambassadors. "Set apart for me Barnabas and Saul for the work to which I have called them" (Acts 13:2). In consequence, the church of Jesus Christ should be a spiritual fellowship, sensitive and knowledgeable, knowing those men and women in their midst who are equipped by God and made willing of God for special service.

Spiritual overseers. Another claimant for this power to give an external call is the bishops and overseers. The general term in scripture is "elders." Elders include bishops, pastors, teachers and presbyters. It is a general term for those holding such offices n the church.

It is quite clear that these elders have a special responsibility under God in such matters. They should lead in things spiritual and be able to discern and recognize the credentials of those who claim to be called. They are to "pay careful attention" both to themselves and to "all the flock in which the Holy Spirit has made you overseers, to care for the church of God" (Acts

20:28). They are to be "guardians over" (*episkopos*), to shepherd the church of God.

The State. My personal conviction is that, since governments of today lay no claim to allegiance to Christ, I see no scriptural warrant for the State to exercise any power or jurisdiction in this spiritual matter. A call to the ministry, whether primarily to believers or unbelievers, and near or far, is essentially:

A call from the head of the church, enabling and making willing.

A call confirmed by Christ's faithful people—both ordinary believers and elders—separating those men and women to the work for which the Holy Spirit has called them.

It will surely be the precursor to the revival for which true Christians pray when the church is made willing to reform her life and her ways solely in accord with the word of God and not by the traditions and customs of any particular association or denomination.

On Missionary Work

Leslie Land's ministry was marked by saying much on the call to the work of the gospel. He mentioned in December 1952 how he had met with 25 young people who were considering a call to missionary work. The numbers of missionaries sent out from Melbourne Hall steadily grew throughout his time. We have seen that some associated with the church were notable figures. John Dean, prominent in Nigeria; Archdeacon "Jack" Sperry working in the Canadian Arctic; George Burton, who was a regular writer in the magazine on the principles of such work in July and October 1954 and at numerous other times.

His outline "Are You Called," a summary of one of his messages, is the previous piece in this volume. We also have seen how the church was at the heart of the church planting venture in Knighton, Leicester, which became marked by a fine ministry under Sidney Lawrence and later Herbert Carson. The first meeting of the new church took place on 14 March 1954, with a core early attendance of 35.

In the second half of his time, he began to think and write about the principles of missionary support. His church held an annual Missionary Convention, and this was always extensively reported in the magazine. There were constant pieces in the magazine from missionaries linked to the church and it was not uncommon for the Sunday morning ministry to be delivered by one of them.

In late November 1955 and again in January 1956, the magazine's main focus was on principles of missionary work, focussing on missionary societies and their relation to the local church. In the final months of his ministry, he wrote a piece on 'Missionary Finance' for the Christian paper "The Life of Faith," that came out March 10, 1960, and was reprinted in the April issue of the church magazine. That article was followed in the same issue of "The Life of Faith" by an appreciative letter from John Savage, the General Secretary of "The Evangelical Union of South America."[1] His sermon outline, "Are You Called," appeared in the June 1960 magazine shortly after the article from "The Life of Faith."[2]

His concerns were expressed most firmly in the 1960 article. The following paragraphs integrate the central parts of what he wrote, and outline his concerns and his response in the light of his understanding of the New Testament, especially the opening verses of Acts 13. While the times in which he ministered were different from today, his concern to understand and apply New Testament principles in this area played a significant part in the deepening of a biblically and historically informed evangelicalism in the UK and more widely from the 1950s onwards.

---

[1] The valuable archives of The Evangelical Union of South America are held at https://archiveshub.jisc.ac.uk/search/archives/fc8c2a0c-bee8-3b1a-87a0-08fdc8fffcc2 The archive notes the "the main fields of operation for EUSA were Peru, Brazil and Argentina. EUSA ran evangelical bookshops, evangelical bible schools and seminaries, medical services, and forged alliances with local evangelical church organisations in order to cement a native-led interdenominational evangelical movement in South America."

[2] "The Life of Faith" was one of the main UK inter-denominational Christian newspapers in the decades before the launch of "Evangelical Times," and sometime later, "Evangelicals Now."

The Missionary Call and the Local Church

The Problem

As a minister of the gospel actively concerned in the sending out of missionaries, I am persuaded that there are far too many freelance, "unchurched" applicants for missionary service. They have little or no link with a local church or fellowship of believers …

Not infrequently nowadays younger Christians in our churches "become missionaries" in a very private, individual-istic way. Quite often the minister and elders of the local church know nothing whatever of the "call" until well after an application has been lodged with some society. The body of be-lievers in the church may know nothing whatever of this all-important matter. There is no *fellowship in prayer* and waiting upon the Lord leading up to the "call."

The Holy Spirit has little opportunity of saying anything to the church.

Our financial problem in missionary work arises largely through confused, woolly thinking which has very largely di-vorced evangelical enterprise from the local fellowship of be-lievers. When and where the local church is revived there will be no finance problem, missionary or otherwise.

Far too many missionary candidates, when asked at an in-terview about their "call," merely refer to some outside meeting they happened to attend; or they refer to a misuse of holy scrip-ture, such as how the bible happened to open one morning at a verse in Jeremiah—a violent form of exegesis with which we are all becoming painfully familiar. There is seldom, all too sel-dom, any reference to a local church given to prayer and fasting or a local church separating, laying-on-hands in token of sacrificial fellowship and *sending* them on their way. It is only later on that fellow-believers are invited to become "prayer partners." Little wonder that the missionary allowances are down. Nobody knows, and so nobody cares.

Despite the commitment of his church to annual missionary conventions, he was aware that these were not enough. Following the 1955 Convention he addressed this question in the following way. [Ed.]

Another Missionary Convention has come to an end. What is our reaction to it all? There will be some who say, "We quite enjoyed the films and the talks." They will compare and contrast them with previous conventions and that is about all. But there may be others—perhaps especially among young people—who will be feeling restless, perhaps even wondering of they ought to give in their notice at the office, the hospital or the factory next week, and go into some kind of missionary training. They do not quite know *why* or *where* they should go, but they have been seized with a vague, uneasy feeling that it is somehow slack and wrong of them to stay where they are.

Indeed, in this frame of mind some are even inclined to look upon their church fellowship with misgivings and apprehension. Perhaps they are enjoying too many spiritual blessings? Perhaps we *all* ought to…? And so, unless we are careful, these conventions which are designed to be a season of blessing to God's people and of glory to God, may prove to be for some a time of mere outward excitement and stimulus. Unless we are prepared to do some serious thinking and waiting upon God, we may even find ourselves taking a step which is far removed from God's call or God's purpose for our lives.

He countered these problems in ways which resulted in the establishment of a church "Missionary Policy" which was set out in the January 1956 issue of the magazine. The core of the policy was to aim at "nothing less than the total support of all our own representatives out on the foreign field." It followed a period when the question of missionary giving had been "vented in prayer meetings (the best and safest place!), Elders Meetings and in the Missionary Committee." It came at a time when Leslie Land could record that the church "soon will have, please God, some half a dozen or more missionaries out in the front line of world evangelisation," a number that continued to grow through the subsequent years of his ministry, to perhaps, the evidence suggests, fourteen at the time he left the church six years after writing the following article. [Ed.]

The Missionary Call

> Now there were in the church at Antioch prophets and
> teachers, Barnabas, Simeon who was called Niger, Lu-
> cius of Cyrene, Manaen a lifelong friend of Herod the
> tetrarch, and Saul. While they were worshiping the Lord
> and fasting, the Holy Spirit said, "Set apart for me Bar-
> nabas and Saul for the work to which I have called
> them." Then after fasting and praying they laid their
> hands on them and sent them off. So, being sent out by
> the Holy Spirit, they went down to Seleucia, and from
> there they sailed to Cyprus. (Acts 13:1–4)

In the opening verses of Acts 13 we see how some of the first
missionaries were called. We find that the Holy Spirit called
these missionaries. "The Holy Spirit said, 'Set apart for me Barnabas and Saul for the work to which *I* have called them.'" Further, we note that the "call" came to these men in *the local
church*. Indeed, the call came to the church as they worshipped,
fasted and prayed. "Set apart for me Barnabas and Saul."

Just *how* the Holy Spirit communicated the will of God to
this church at Antioch we do not know. I do not think for one
moment he wrote it in the sky or revealed God's purposes to
them in a magical way. I think He impressed it firmly, steadily,
clearly upon the hearts and wills of Barnabas and Saul that the
Lord had a great purpose for their lives in the "regions beyond." But more than that, it seems clear that the Holy Spirit
also revealed His choice to the church. God's worshipping people at Antioch in Syria had come to know and feel that

Barnabas and Saul were utterly consecrated men whom God was about to thrust out into a wider ministry. The church was agreed and definitely involved in this "call."

Looking again at the Antioch church, it was here that the disciples were first called "Christians" (Acts 11:26). It was a delightful, very mixed fellowship, with many spiritual gifts and abilities. There was Joseph Barnabas, John Mark's uncle, a "good man," full of the Holy Spirit and faith. There was Simon Niger, a black man who had found Christ and was now a member and a teacher of the church at Antioch. Then there was Lucius from Cyrene, who was a Gentile, and Manaen who had been part of the court of King Herod. Then there was Saul of Tarsus, the Pharisee. It was a miracle of grace that brought such men together and united them in Christ.

The church at Antioch was a spiritually-minded, praying church. Their love for Christ also led them to love their fellowmen. They had already had a gift-day for the needy Christians in Judea. It was to this church, as they worshipped and prayed, that the missionary call came, and from God, not the minister or teachers. It did not come to all of them, but to two, but all were involved with the two. The two were an integral part of the whole, for it was the *church* that separated itself ("fasted") and prayed; the *church* laid hands on God's called ones as an outward sign and seal of the fellowship's oneness in the gospel in the thrusting out of these two men. The laying on of hands must not be confused with ordination, for they already had received their "divine orders." They were teachers and preachers of the word.

The church prayed with them and sent them away, and yet it was the Holy Spirit who really sent them *through the church*. "They laid their hands on them and sent them off. So, being sent out by the Holy Spirit, they went." The church at home went with them in prayer, in fellowship and (you may be sure) in giving. There was no serious missionary problem in the church at Antioch. The Holy Spirit was free to communicate his will to a people who were united in service and waiting upon God.

The missionary call is still the Holy Spirit's prerogative. He still does it through the church when and where that church truly *is* a church. Are we near enough to Christ and therefore to each other for the Holy Spirit to be able to say, "Set apart for me so-and-so for the work to which I have called them"?

Appendix
Bible Passages and Texts
on which Leslie Land Preached

Book	Passages	Number of occasions
Genesis		
Exodus	Ch. 3; 12:26–27; Ch. 20	3
Leviticus		
Numbers		
Deut		
Joshua	1:1–5; 3:4	2
Judges	2:10	1
Ruth		
1 Samuel		
2 Samuel	5:22–25	1
1 Kings		
2 Kings		
1 Chronicles		
2 Chronicles		
Ezra		
Nehemiah		
Esther	Overview	1
Job		
Psalms	34:5; 130:4; 145:10	3
Proverbs	3:5–6	1
Ecclesiastes	7:6	1
Song of Songs	4:12–16	1
Isaiah	Ch. 1–31; Ch. 2; Ch. 5; 10:15 ("Axes and Saws"); 40:3–5; 54.:2	7
Jeremiah	2:13	1
Lamantations		
Ezekiel		
Daniel		

Hosea	6:3	1
Joel		
Amos		
Obadiah		
Jonah		
Micah		
Nahum		
Habakuk		
Zephaniah		
Haggai		
Zechariah		
Malachi	Ch. 4.	1
	Old Testament Total	24
Matthew	1:18; 2.:2; 5:8; 6:33; 7:1–5; 13:13; 14:18	7
Mark		
Luke	3:1–2 [twice]; 3:4–6; 7:38; 10:39; 11:29–36; 12:19; 15:2; 17:32	9
John	1:1; 1:45; 3:6; 6:37; 6:39–40; 6:44, 54 [v. 44 twice]; 6:65; 8:51 [twice but on different themes]; 12:3; 14:9; 14:27; 15:1–6; 17:18	15
Acts	3:1–4; 4:12; 20:35; Ch. 27	4
Romans	Ch. 1; 6:11; 8:5; 8:29–30; 12;12	5
1 Corinthians	Ch. 1 [twice]; 1:21; 2:1–5; 3:23; 9:21; 11:28	7
2 Corinthians	4:7; 5:16–17	2
Galatians	1:4	1
Ephesians	1:4; 3:3–4; 3:4	3
Philippians	3:7–8; 3:10; 3:20–21	3
Colossians	2:14	1
1 Thessalonians		
2 Thessalonians		
1 Timothy		
2 Timothy	3:1–5, 14; 3:16	2
Titus		
Philemon		
Hebrews	3:7; 9:28; 10:19–25; 11:13–16; 12:2	5

James	3:6; 4:1-2	2
1 Peter	1;13; 3:18; 3:20; 5:7	4
2 Peter		
1 John	1:7; 2:15–17; 3:1–2; 3:2; 5:11–12	5
2 John		
3 John	2	1
Jude		
Revelation	Overview; 1:5–6; 6:15–17	3
	New Testament total	79

Notes

1. This does not include 1956–1959.
2. This is not a profile of the passages on which he preached. It is a record of the parts of the bible he drew on when having in view the readership of the monthly magazine. This magazine went out beyond the immediate congregation and was distributed to (an unknown number of) homes in Leicester. This probably accounts for the strong evangelistic emphasis in the overall balance.
3. The month by month passages chosen do not tell us how he handled the expository dimension of his ministry. It was the case that he used the weeknight Bible School as a vehicle for expository series, when he would work through books of the bible such as Romans and Daniel, and give extended series on topics such as "Books of the Bible." These are not included here.
4. Almost 77% of magazine texts were from the New Testament [79/103]. Of these 55 were from the gospels—a remarkable figure. Almost 70% of the New Testament texts he chose for the magazine were from the gospels and of the whole, 53% of times he opted for a gospel text.

5. The number of instances occasionally does not match number of cited texts, because he would sometimes treat texts from two parts of the bible.

Acknowledgements

I thank Dr. Brian Beardsworth for first drawing my attention to the relationship between Land and Lloyd-Jones. Iain Murray for loaning me the collection of the twenty-seven surviving letters from Lloyd-Jones to Land, between 1938 and 1957, and for help in deciphering some of 'The Doctor's' bewildering handwriting. Three of the letters found their way into Iain Murray's 1994 book, *D. Martyn Lloyd-Jones. Letters 1919-1981.* Edinburgh: Banner of Truth Trust.

The late Kathryn Land for writing to me and entrusting me with her husband's annotated, heavily underlined bible and samples of his sermon notes. Joscelyn Johnson filled in invaluable details about Land's period at Seaford College. I am also grateful to Mary Ward for bound copies of the Melbourne Hall Magazine covering most of Leslie Land's ministry, and to his nephew Ian Land, Jonathan Catherwood and various people for their memories and encouragement in excavating this lost story. Lady Elizabeth Catherwood made helpful comments on an earlier draft of Chapter Two.

Finally, to my wife, Maria, for undertaking the greater part of the transcription of Leslie Land's messages.

Permissions
I am grateful to the following for permission to reprint the following articles. The articles by the author have been further edited.
Banner of Truth Trust, Edinburgh.
Shaw, Ian. "A Christian friendship: Martyn Lloyd-Jones and Leslie Land." *Banner of Truth Magazine* Issue 604, 2014.

Land, W. Leslie. "The Earnest of our inheritance," *Banner of Truth Magazine,* April 2020.

Reformation Today for:

Shaw, Ian. "A Leicester Awakening," *Reformation Today* #268, 2015.

Shaw, Ian. "Leslie Land: a Christian Ministry," *Reformation Today* #269 2016

Shaw, Ian, "Leslie Land: a Preaching Ministry," *Reformation Today* #270, 2016.

Land, W. Leslie. "Are you called?" *Reformation Today.* #295, 2020.

Land, W. Leslie. "Hegemony," *Reformation Today.* #295, 2020.

Jonathan Catherwood, for the photograph of Dr Martyn Lloyd-Jones

"Loving His Appearing" first appeared in the privately published book, Land, W. Leslie, *The Appearing of Jesus* Second edition. York Publishing Services, 2014.

Index

Index